THE PRINCE

THE PRINCE

Niccolò Machiavelli

*Supplementary material written by
Benjamin Beard
Series edited by Cynthia Brantley Johnson*

POCKET BOOKS
NEW YORK LONDON TORONTO SYDNEY

POCKET BOOKS, a division of Simon & Schuster, Inc.
1230 Avenue of the Americas, New York, NY 10020

Supplementary materials copyright © 2004 by Simon & Schuster, Inc.

ISBN13: 978-0-7434-8768-9
ISBN10: 0-7434-8768-0

First Pocket Books printing July 2004

10 9 8 7 6 5 4 3 2

POCKET and colophon are registered trademarks of Simon & Schuster, Inc.

Cover design by Jeanne M. Lee
Cover illustration by Marco Ventura

Manufactured in the United States of America

For information regarding special discounts for bulk purchases, please contact Simon & Schuster Special Sales at 1-800-456-6798 or business@simonandschuster.com.

CONTENTS

INTRODUCTION

THE PRINCE: A PRIMER IN POWER POLITICS

Italian thinker Niccolò Machiavelli's reputation rests almost solely on *The Prince,* a short political tract written in 1513 that advises ruling figures on how to govern. Machiavelli thought the book would stay relevant for fewer than ten years. Nearly five hundred years have now passed since the book was first penned, and it seems just as current now as it did then. Without question, *The Prince* has had a huge impact on international politics. It has provoked anger, sparked debate, and influenced scores of historical leaders—both petty and grand. But Machiavelli's original intentions, and an uncontested understanding of the book's meaning, have eluded readers since its initial publication.

The Prince's structure is simple: a series of chapters, each advising a new ruler on how to deal with a specific situation. The advice is aimed at a type of ruler that was fairly new in fifteenth- and sixteenth-century Italy, a "prince" (Machiavelli uses this term to refer to any head of state) whose power lay not in history, tradition, or custom but rather in military power, money, and ambition. Machiavelli illustrates his points with examples from history and uses the failings and successes of the great rulers of ancient times—such as Philip of Macedon, Hannibal of Carthage, and Alexander the Great—to bolster his arguments. Machiavelli explains how to deal with foreign occupations, how to make a conquered people love you, how to tax, how to allocate offices, how to succeed. He explains how to gain glory, how to advance your country's power—ultimately, how to be a strong ruler. Many of the situations he describes are still faced by today's corporate and political leaders, one of the main reasons the book still seems so current.

But being a ruler, Machiavelli explains, also requires deceit and cruelty, and he offers copious justification and practical advice for employing craft and terror in political dealings. Seemingly unconcerned with the moral consequences of his ideas, Machiavelli tells the new ruler how to accomplish his goals, and does not hide the brutality and violence that must sometimes accompany a campaign for power. In fact, *The Prince* seems to endorse totalitarianism, and Machiavelli seems to recommend tyrants, oligarchies, and military regimes over democratic governments. It is this facet of *The Prince* that has caused Machiavelli's name to become synonymous with amoral politics.

But was Machiavelli writing of the world as it was, or the world as he thought it should be? Was he simply describing the status quo, or laying out a program for maximum efficiency? Was he being serious or satirical? Did he believe in what he was writing, or did he simply say what the ruling family of Florence wanted to hear? Was

Machiavelli a political realist or an advocate of absolute amorality? These questions should be kept in mind when reading *The Prince,* as they remain largely unanswered to this day.

Historical Context of *The Prince*: An Outline of the Italian Renaissance

Machiavelli lived during the Italian Renaissance, a time of unparalleled artistic, scientific, and philosophical achievement. Leonardo da Vinci, Michelangelo, and Machiavelli are just three of the hundreds of important artists and thinkers working in the time period. The invention of the movable-type printing press in 1455 had made books easier and cheaper to print, causing an explosion in writing as well as publishing and wide circulation of new philosophical and scientific thought. But this intellectual progress took place amid great political and religious upheaval. The absolute power of the Roman Catholic Church in Europe was weakening, in large part because of popular disgust over the sensuality and decadence of some of the popes. To support their lavish courts, several popes used the sale of indulgences to raise money. Popularized by Pope Sixtus IV, the selling of indulgences refers to the practice of charging churchgoers money for the remission of their sins (though this is not, according to Catholic doctrine, how indulgences are supposed to be used).

In 1478, Pope Sixtus IV authorized the Spanish Inquisition with the intention of rooting out the unfaithful in Spain. Suspected heretics and infidels were rounded up and tortured into submission or confession. It was a dark, intolerant, superstitious period in the history of

Christianity that stretched until the early nineteenth century (when the Inquisition was formally ended by decree). During this time, many thousands of accused heretics were burned alive at the stake and maimed by unspeakable tortures.

Despite such terrifying deterrents, clergy and common folk across Europe began to voice their dissatisfaction with the Church, and various non-Catholic Christian sects sprang up. In 1517, Martin Luther, a German monk, inadvertently started the Protestant Reformation when he nailed his famous "Ninety-Five Theses," a tract decrying the sale of indulgences, to the door of the church in the town of Wittenberg. Luther's act ushered in hundreds of years of violent religious wars in which Catholics and Protestants slaughtered one another and the exact terms of one's religious faith became a life-and-death issue. Understandably, since the constantly changing political landscape brought various religious beliefs in and out of favor and almost anyone could be denounced as a heretic on almost any pretext, an atmosphere of fear, hysteria, and paranoia dominated much of Europe.

The political landscape of Italy was just as fractious as the religious landscape of Europe. Italy as a nation did not exist until the nineteenth century. In Machiavelli's time, Italy was composed of squabbling city-states, each with its own ruler, battling over land on the Italian peninsula. The five dominant powers—Milan, the Kingdom of Naples, Venice, the Papal States, and Florence—jockeyed over land and influence, constantly forming then breaking alliances with one another.

Milan was dominated by the Visconti family—a

vengeful, aggressive clan that ruled Milan for more than a hundred years and controlled much of northwest Italy. Milan was a wealthy, extravagant place. Eventually, Francesco Sforza, the treacherous soldier much talked about in *The Prince*, took over. Milan, like many of the Italian city-states, experienced numerous changes in government, including a ten-year occupation by the French.

After Milan, Venice was the second strongest power in Italy and one of the oldest existing republics. The city-state was ruled by regularly elected doges, with the strong natural defense of the sea protecting it. Venice had the relative peace it needed to become a thriving city of craftsmen, selling products all over the known world through a lucrative shipping trade. Venice was a powerful, majestic place and, for its time, progressive in its politics.

The Kingdom of Naples was a highly contested region, rich in port cities and land, with monarchs all over Europe laying claim to its throne. The Papal States were the collective cities owned by the Roman Catholic Church. Powerful landowners with the wealth and influence of the Church behind them exploited the power of the temporal authority of heaven that the Church represented.

And then there was Florence, Machiavelli's home and a thriving, business-oriented, mercantile state, which had been dominated by the Medici family until they were expelled by the people and the republic was formed. The Florentine republic was a fast-paced, exciting place, with regular elections. To keep ambitious politicians from accumulating too much personal power, the Florentines kept terms of office very short— some terms were as short as two months. Unfortunately, this lack of continuity hurt the government, as no stable infrastructures could develop under such conditions.

An uneasy equilibrium existed among the five powers, as none was strong enough to conquer the other four. The balance was precarious. Each state at one point or another desired the wealth of its Italian neighbors. Further jeopardizing the balance of power was the fact that Italy was surrounded by strong, centralized countries with large standing armies—countries such as France, Germany, and Spain. The Italian city-states relied on mercenary armies in their conflicts, which were expensive and often hard to control.

The Italians all considered themselves Italian. They all spoke the same language, more or less. They were all Roman Catholic (publicly, at least). They recognized the sanctity of the Italian borders. They resented the interference of outside countries. But the Italians could not agree on who should rule over a unified Italy or what type of government an Italian nation should have. This problem would plague Italy for centuries.

In Machiavelli's opinion, Italy's best hope for a unifying leader was Cesare Borgia, a strong, ambitious man who was a capable military commander. Cesare's father, Alexander VI, was the pope, and together they had plans to unify, and then control, Italy.

In 1502, King Louis XII of France, at the bidding of Pope Alexander VI, backed Cesare Borgia's military campaign to unify Italy. Louis owed Alexander a favor because Alexander had granted Louis a divorce in 1498 so he could marry Anne of Brittany and maintain the unity of Brittany and France. At first, Alexander and Cesare's plan worked; with the French army supporting him, Cesare began accumulating land in the area of Italy known as Romagna. But fortune turned against Cesare, as his father died unexpectedly and Cesare grew sick. The result was a French army, too strong for any individual Italian city-state to defeat, in control of half of Naples and all of Milan. Spain got involved, attacking the French and eventually gaining control of Naples for itself. So Cesare's attempt to gain control over Italy ended with two foreign armies, and innumerable foreign mercenaries, running rampant up and down the Italian peninsula.

The Italian Wars—the collective term for the series of campaigns by Spain, France, and the Holy Roman Empire to take over parts of Italy—lasted until 1559. The wars spread the intellectual and artistic advances of the Italian Renaissance throughout the rest of Europe, but they were disastrous for Italy, with a particularly low point in Italian history coming in 1527, the year of Machiavelli's death. A grumbling army of underpaid mercenaries under the banner of the Holy Roman Empire took control of Rome and spent months sacking the city—plundering, raping, murdering, and maiming—while the defenseless Italian people could only watch in horror. This effectively ended the Italian Renaissance. Italy, the religious, and for a time intellectual, center of the Western world, was utterly devastated. It would be centuries before the country could pull itself back together.

The Life and Work of Niccolò Machiavelli

Niccolò de Bernardo Machiavelli was born on May 3, 1469, to a middle-class Florentine family. Although his

family had a good record with public office, his father
was neither successful nor wealthy. Instead, he offered
his son a wealth of knowledge in books—an education
in the classics that Machiavelli would put to good use.

In 1498, during the exile of the Medici family from
Florence, Machiavelli was elected to the office of Chancellor to the Second Chancery, acting as a mid-level bureaucrat who dealt with correspondence and other
matters of state, an office he would hold for fourteen
years. During his role as chancellor, he met some important persons of the day, including Pope Julius II and
the Holy Roman Emperor Maximilian I. Machiavelli's
views on governing bodies and municipal politics were
thus formed by both his classical education and his experience in the trenches of the Florentine bureaucracy.
He saw firsthand the advantages of having a country
united behind a strong ruler.

Early on in his career, he campaigned for the raising
of a standing Florentine army. He eventually was given
the job of creating a militia, and began gathering an
army for the defense of Florence. When the Medicis
returned in 1512, backed by the powerful Spanish
army, Machiavelli's troops broke and ran. The Florentine republic was abolished, and Machiavelli was humil-
iated, both publicly and privately.

On February 12, 1513, Machiavelli was arrested by
the Medicis and tortured for his possible involvement
in an anti-Medici plot. He was then forced into retirement, where he lived in the countryside and began
composing *The Prince*. Although the fall of the Florentine republic was a personal failure for Machiavelli, it
fired his political and authorial imagination. It was during his retirement that he created his entire literary

oeuvre: *The Discourses on Livy, The Mandrake Root,* and *The Art of War,* among others.

Machiavelli was an enthusiastic letter writer, and much of his correspondence remains intact. From his personal writings, a witty, dramatic personality emerges, and it is clear that he enjoyed portraying himself as a rogue and relished the role of the villain. He was a fiercely independent thinker who used strong, clear prose, two qualities that set him apart even from the other intellectuals of the Italian Renaissance. His unapologetic pragmatism has led many historians to label him amoral, if not outright evil, but this is precisely why he is worth reading. The fact that he recognized the need to acknowledge those in power is seen by many as a weakness; however, he probably would have scoffed at the accusation.

His personal beliefs are hard to grasp. He wrote both *The Prince,* seen by many as a protofascist defense of totalitariansm, and *Discourses on Livy,* one of the first modern treatises on republics. This mercurial, almost chameleonlike ability to write convincingly about opposing philosophies of government is confounding. On the one hand, it may be seen as moral weakness; on the other hand, it may be a sign of mental flexibility.

Eventually, Machiavelli was given a small job by the Medicis, to write the history of Florence. Unfortunately, he was once again the victim of unfortunate timing and political upheaval; the Medicis were expelled again. Machiavelli was exuberant and applied for his old post, but the republic officials refused, seeing his behavior as duplicitous. The spark in Machiavelli went out, as the republic he valued so much had spurned him.

Machiavelli never attained the greatness of office that he desired, nor was he ever in a position to enact the principles of leadership about which he wrote. He witnessed many of the great personages and events of his time period but had little influence on them. In June 1527, he grew ill, suffering spasms of the stomach. He confessed to a priest, then died, twelve days later. His last words are supposed to have been: "I desire to go to hell and not to heaven. In the former place I shall enjoy the company of popes, kings, and princes, while in the latter are only beggars, monks, and apostles." To the last, he desired to be in the presence of great men.

On his grave, the monument reads: "No eulogy would do justice to so great a name." Virtually unknown in his lifetime, he now resides at the front of political thought. After his death, he achieved the fame, stature, and influence that in his lifetime he so longed for.

CHRONOLOGY OF NICCOLÒ MACHIAVELLI'S LIFE AND WORK

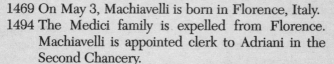

1469 On May 3, Machiavelli is born in Florence, Italy.

1494 The Medici family is expelled from Florence. Machiavelli is appointed clerk to Adriani in the Second Chancery.

1498 Adriani becomes chancellor, and Machiavelli succeeds him as second chancellor and secretary.

1500 Machiavelli is sent to France, where he meets with Louis XII and the cardinal of Rouen.

1502 Machiavelli marries Marietta Corsini. He is sent to Romagna as envoy to Cesare Borgia, where he witnesses the events leading up to Borgia's murder.

1503 In January, Machiavelli returns to Florence.

1504 Machiavelli's second mission to France.

1506 In December, Machiavelli submits a plan to reorganize the Florentine military, and it is accepted.

1508 He is sent to Bolzano to the court of the Emperor Maximilian.

1510 Machiavelli's third mission to France.

1512 The Medicis return to Florence with a Spanish army and retake control of the city. Machiavelli is dismissed from office, and he retires to San Casciano.

1513 Machiavelli is imprisoned and tortured after being accused of conspiracy. Once released, he returns to San Casciano and writes *The Prince*.

1515 Machiavelli writes *La Mandragola (The Mandrake Root)*.

1519 Machiavelli is consulted by the Medicis for a new constitution for Florence, which he offers in his *Discourses*.

1520 Machiavelli finishes *The Art of War* and *The Life of Castruccio Castracane*. He is commissioned to write the *History of Florence*.

1526 Clement VII employs Machiavelli as secretary of a five-man body constituted to inspect the fortifications of Florence.

1527 The Medicis are expelled again. Machiavelli applies for his old post but is refused. On June 20, Machiavelli dies of an illness in Florence.

HISTORICAL CONTEXT OF *The Prince*

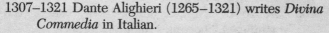

1307–1321 Dante Alighieri (1265–1321) writes *Divina Commedia* in Italian.

1341 Petrarch crowned poet laureate of Italy, an event sometimes considered the start of the Italian Renaissance.

1347–1351 The Bubonic Plague sweeps through Italy and Europe, killing between a quarter and one half of the population.

1348–1353 Giovanni Boccaccio (1313–1375) writes the *Decameron*, stories set during the period of the Black Plague, in Italian.

1366 Petrarch (1304–1374), writing in both Latin and Italian, produces *Canzoniere* in Italian, a model for sonnet form.

1412 Filippo Brunelleschi (1377–1446) writes *Rules of Perspective*. In 1419, he designs the octagonal ribbed cupola of the Florence cathedral.

1420 The papacy returns to Rome, having been located in Avignon since 1305.

1434 Cosimo de' Medici (1389–1464) becomes ruler of Florence.

1440 Platonic Academy founded in Florence.

1450 After a short experiment with republican government, Milan returns to monarchy when Francesco Sforza takes control of the city. His most prominent successor is Ludovico Sforza.

1453 Constantinople, center of Eastern Church and Byzantine Empire, falls to the Turks. Scholars flee to Italy bringing Greek manuscripts, further fueling the Renaissance.

1455 Johannes Gutenberg (1400–1468), a German, prints a copy of the Bible using a printing press set with movable type.

1469 Lorenzo de' Medici (1389–1464), called "the Magnificent," becomes ruler of Florence.

1471 Sixtus IV becomes pope, undertaking many successful projects in Rome but disgracing the Church through his corruption and practice of nepotism.

1475 Cesare Borgia born.

1484 Sandro Botticelli (1444–1510) paints *The Birth of Venus* for the Medici family.

1492 Christopher Columbus (1451–1506), sent by King Ferdinand of Spain to the West Indies, accidentally discovers America. Alexander VI, the notorious Borgia pope (father of Cesare Borgia), becomes pope.

1494 Giovanni Pico della Mirandola (1463–1494) publishes *The Dignity of Man*, considered a major statement of Renaissance humanism.

1494 Charles VIII, king of France, invades the Italian peninsula at the request of Lodovico Sforza, taking Naples. This signals the end of independence for the Italian city-states.

1494 Dominican friar Girolamo Savonarola leads an uprising that expels the Medicis from Florence, installing a puritanical regime.

1498 Savonarola is excommunicated and hanged.

1503 Leonardo da Vinci (1452–1519), Florentine painter, sculptor, architect, engineer, weapons designer, and scientist, begins painting *Mona Lisa*.

1503 Pope Alexander VI dies. Cesare Borgia grows ill, and his military campaign in the Romagna falters. Julius II becomes pope.

1507 Death of Cesare Borgia.

1508–1512 Michelangelo (1475–1564), sculptor, painter, architect, and poet, paints the ceiling of the Sistine Chapel in Rome.

1512 The Medici family is restored to power in Florence.

1513 Giovanni de' Medici is elected Pope Leo X. He becomes a great patron of the arts. Rome prospers under Leo's rule.

1513 Machiavelli writes *The Prince*.

1517 The Protestant Reformation movement begins when Martin Luther posts his "Ninety-Five Theses" on the door of a church in Wittenberg, Germany. Results in a huge split in the Catholic Church.

1519 Leonardo da Vinci dies in France.

1527 Sack of Rome. Machiavelli dies.

THE PRINCE

Dedication[1]

To the Magnificent Lorenzo di Piero de' Medici

IT IS customary for such as seek a Prince's favour, to present themselves before him with those things of theirs which they themselves most value, or in which they perceive him chiefly to delight. Accordingly, we often see horses, armour, cloth of gold, precious stones, and the like costly gifts, offered to Princes as worthy of their greatness. Desiring in like manner to approach your Magnificence with some token of my devotion, I have found among my possessions none that I so much prize and esteem as a knowledge of the actions of great men, acquired in the course of a long experience of modern affairs and a continual study of antiquity. Which knowledge most carefully and patiently pondered over and sifted by me, and now reduced into this little book, I send to your Magnificence. And though I deem the work unworthy of your greatness, yet am I bold enough to hope that your courtesy will dispose you to accept it, considering that I can offer you no better gift than the means of mastering in a very brief time, all that in the course of so many years, and at the cost of so many hardships and dangers, I have learned, and know.

This work I have not adorned or amplified with rounded periods, swelling and high-flown language, or any other of those extrinsic attractions and allurements wherewith many authors are wont to set off and grace their writings; since it is my desire that it should either pass wholly unhonoured, or that the truth of its matter and the importance of its subject should alone recommend it.

Nor would I have it thought presumption that a person of very mean and humble station should venture to discourse and lay down rules concerning the government of Princes. For as those who make maps of countries place themselves low down in the plains to study the character of mountains and elevated lands, and place themselves high up on the mountains to get a better view of the plains, so in like manner to understand the People a man should be a Prince, and to have a clear notion of Princes he should belong to the People.

Let your Magnificence, then, accept this little gift in the spirit in which I offer it; wherein, if you diligently read and study it, you will recognize my extreme desire that you should attain to that eminence which Fortune and your own merits promise you. Should you from the height of your greatness some time turn your eyes to these humble regions, you will become aware how undeservedly I have to endure the keen and unremitting malignity of Fortune.

Chapter I

OF THE VARIOUS KINDS OF PRINCEDOM, AND OF THE WAYS IN WHICH THEY ARE ACQUIRED

A LL THE STATES and Governments by which men are or ever have been ruled, have been and are either Republics or Princedoms. Princedoms are either hereditary, in which the sovereignty is derived through an ancient line of ancestors, or they are new. New Princedoms are either wholly new, as that of Milan to Francesco Sforza;[1] or they are like limbs joined on to the hereditary possessions of the Prince who acquires them, as the Kingdom of Naples[2] to the dominions of the King of Spain. The States thus acquired have either been used to live under a Prince or have been free; and he who acquires them does so either by his own arms or by the arms of others, and either by good fortune or by merit.

Chapter II

OF HEREDITARY PRINCEDOMS

O F REPUBLICS I shall not now speak, having elsewhere spoken[1] of them at length. Here I shall treat
exclusively of Princedoms, and, filling in the outline
above traced out, shall proceed to examine how such
States are to be governed and maintained.

I say, then, that hereditary States, accustomed to the
family of their Prince, are maintained with far less difficulty than new States, since all that is required is that
the Prince shall not depart from the usages of his ancestors, trusting for the rest to deal with events as they
arise. So that if an hereditary Prince be of average address, he will always maintain himself in his Princedom,
unless deprived of it by some extraordinary and irre-
sistible force; and even if so deprived will recover it,
should any, even the least, mishap overtake the usurper.
We have in Italy an example of this in the Duke of Ferrara, who never could have withstood the attacks of the
Venetians in 1484, nor those of Pope Julius in 1510,[2]
had not his authority in that State been consolidated by

time. For since a Prince by birth has fewer occasions and less need to give offence, he ought to be better loved, and will naturally be popular with his subjects unless outrageous vices make him odious. Moreover, the very antiquity and continuance of his rule will efface the memories and causes which lead to innovation. For one change always leaves a dovetail into which another will fit.

Chapter III

OF MIXED PRINCEDOMS

BUT IN NEW Princedoms difficulties abound. And, first, if the Princedom be not wholly new, but joined on to the ancient dominions of the Prince, so as to form with them what may be termed a mixed Princedom, changes will come from a cause common to all new States, namely, that men, thinking to better their condition, are always ready to change masters, and in this expectation will take up arms against any ruler; wherein they deceive themselves, and find afterwards by experience that they are worse off than before. This again results naturally and necessarily from the circumstance that the Prince cannot avoid giving offence to his new subjects, either in respect of the troops he quarters on them, or of some other of the numberless vexations attendant on a new acquisition. And in this way you may find that you have enemies in all those whom you have injured in seizing the Princedom, yet cannot keep the friendship of those who helped you to gain it; since you can neither reward

them as they expect, nor yet, being under obligations to them, use violent remedies against them. For however strong you may be in respect of your army, it is essential that in entering a new Province you should have the good will of its inhabitants.

Hence it happened that Louis XII of France, speedily gaining possession of Milan, as speedily lost it; and that on the occasion of its first capture, Lodovico Sforza was able with his own forces only to take it from him. For the very people who had opened the gates to the French King, when they found themselves deceived in their expectations and hopes of future benefits, could not put up with the insolence of their new ruler.[1] True it is that when a State rebels and is again got under, it will not afterwards be lost so easily. For the Prince, using the rebellion as a pretext, will not scruple to secure himself by punishing the guilty, bringing the suspected to trial, and otherwise strengthening his position in the points where it was weak. So that if to recover Milan from the French it was enough on the first occasion that a Duke Lodovico should raise alarms on the frontiers, to wrest it from them a second time the whole world had to be ranged against them, and their armies destroyed and driven out of Italy.[2] And this for the reasons above assigned. And yet, for a second time, Milan was lost to the King. The general causes of its first loss have been shown. It remains to note the causes of the second, and to point out the remedies which the French King had, or which might have been used by another in like circumstances to maintain his conquest more successfully than he did.

I say, then, that those States which upon their acquisition are joined on to the ancient dominions of the

Prince who acquires them, are either of the same Province and tongue as the people of these dominions, or they are not. When they are, there is a great ease in retaining them, especially when they have not been accustomed to live in freedom. To hold them securely it is enough to have rooted out the line of the reigning Prince; because if in other respects the old condition of things be continued, and there be no discordance in their customs, men live peaceably with one another, as we see to have been the case in Brittany, Burgundy, Gascony, and Normandy,[3] which have so long been united to France. For although there be some slight difference in their languages, their customs are similar, and they can easily get on together. He, therefore, who acquires such a State, if he mean to keep it, must see to two things; first, that the blood of the ancient line of Princes be destroyed; second, that no change be made in respect of laws or taxes; for in this way the newly acquired State speedily becomes incorporated with the hereditary.

But when States are acquired in a country differing in language, usages, and laws, difficulties multiply, and great good fortune, as well as address, is needed to overcome them. One of the best and most efficacious methods for dealing with such a State, is for the Prince who acquires it to go and dwell there in person, since this will tend to make his tenure more secure and lasting. This course has been followed by the Turk[4] with regard to Greece, who, had he not, in addition to all his other precautions for securing that Province, himself come to live in it, could never have kept his hold of it. For when you are on the spot, disorders are detected in their beginnings and remedies can be readily applied;

but when you are at a distance, they are not heard of until they have gathered strength and the case is past cure. Moreover, the Province in which you take up your abode is not pillaged by your officers; the people are pleased to have a ready recourse to their Prince; and have all the more reason if they are well disposed, to love, if disaffected, to fear him. A foreign enemy desiring to attack that State would be cautious how he did so. In short, where the Prince resides in person, it will be extremely difficult to oust him.

Another excellent expedient is to send colonies into one or two places, so that these may become, as it were, the keys of the Province; for you must either do this, or else keep up a numerous force of men-at-arms and foot soldiers. A Prince need not spend much on colonies. He can send them out and support them at little or no charge to himself, and the only persons to whom he gives offence are those whom he deprives of their fields and houses to bestow them on the new inhabitants. Those who are thus injured form but a small part of the community, and remaining scattered and poor can never become dangerous. All others being left unmolested, are in consequence easily quieted, and at the same time are afraid to make a false move, lest they share the fate of those who have been deprived of their possessions. In few words, these colonies cost less than soldiers, are more faithful, and give less offence, while those who are offended, being, as I have said, poor and dispersed, cannot hurt. And let it here be noted that men are either to be kindly treated, or utterly crushed, since they can revenge lighter injuries, but not graver. Wherefore the injury we do to a man should be of a sort to leave no fear of reprisals.

But if instead of colonies you send troops, the cost is vastly greater, and the whole revenues of the country are spent in guarding it; so that the gain becomes a loss, and much deeper offence is given; since in shifting the quarters of your soldiers from place to place the whole country suffers hardship, which as all feel, all are made enemies; and enemies who remaining, although vanquished, in their own homes, have power to hurt. In every way, therefore, this mode of defence is as disadvantageous as that by colonizing is useful.

The Prince who establishes himself in a Province whose laws and language differ from those of his own people, ought also to make himself the head and protector of his feebler neighbours, and endeavour to weaken the stronger, and must see that by no accident shall any other stranger as powerful as himself find an entrance there. For it will always happen that some such person will be called in by those of the Province who are discontented either through ambition or fear; as we see of old the Romans brought into Greece by the Aetolians,[5] and in every other country that they entered, invited there by its inhabitants. And the usual course of things is that so soon as a formidable stranger enters a Province, all the weaker powers side with him, moved thereto by the ill-will they bear towards him who has hitherto kept them in subjection. So that in respect of these lesser powers, no trouble is needed to gain them over, for at once, together, and of their own accord, they throw in their lot with the government of the stranger. The new Prince, therefore, has only to see that they do not increase too much in strength, and with his own forces, aided by their good will, can easily subdue any who are powerful, so as to remain supreme in the Province. He who does not manage this matter well, will soon lose whatever he has gained, and while he retains it will find in it endless troubles and annoyances.

In dealing with the countries of which they took possession the Romans diligently followed the methods I have described. They planted colonies, conciliated weaker powers without adding to their strength, humbled the great, and never suffered a formidable stranger to acquire influence. A single example will suffice to show this. In Greece the Romans took the Achaians and Aetolians into their pay; the Macedonian monarchy was humbled; Antiochus was driven out. But the services of the Achaians and Aetolians never obtained for them any addition to their power; no persuasions on the part of Philip could induce the Romans to be his friends on the condition of sparing him humiliation; nor could all the power of Antiochus bring them to consent to his exercising any authority within that Province.[6] And in thus acting the Romans did as all wise rulers should, who have to consider not only present difficulties but also future, against which they must use all diligence to provide; for these, if they be foreseen while yet remote, admit of easy remedy, but if their approach be awaited, are already past cure, the disorder having become hopeless; realizing what the physicians tell us of hectic fever, that in its beginning it is easy to cure, but hard to recognize; whereas, after a time, not having been detected and treated at the first, it becomes easy to recognize but impossible to cure.

And so it is with State affairs. For the distempers of a State being discovered while yet inchoate, which can only be done by a sagacious ruler, may easily be dealt with; but when, from not being observed, they are suffered to grow until they are obvious to every one, there is no longer any remedy. The Romans, therefore, foreseeing evils while they were yet far off, always provided against them, and never suffered them to take their course for the sake of avoiding war; since they knew that war is not so to be avoided, but is only postponed to the advantage of the other side. They chose, therefore, to make war with Philip and Antiochus in Greece, that they might not have to make it with them in Italy, although for a while they might have escaped both. This they did not desire, nor did the maxim *leave it to Time,* which the wise men of our own day have always on their lips, ever recommend itself to them. What they looked to enjoy were the fruits of their own valour and foresight. For Time, driving all things before it, may bring with it evil as well as good.

But let us now go back to France and examine whether she has followed any of those methods of which I have made mention. I shall speak of Louis and not of Charles, because from the former having held longer possession of Italy,[7] his manner of acting is more plainly seen.[8] You will find, then, that he has done the direct opposite of what he should have done in order to retain a foreign State.

King Louis was brought into Italy by the ambition of the Venetians, who hoped by his coming to gain for themselves a half of the State of Lombardy. I will not blame this coming, nor the part taken by the King, because, desiring to gain a footing in Italy, where he had no friends, but on the contrary, owing to the conduct of Charles, every door was shut against him, he was driven to accept such friendships as he could get. And his designs might easily have succeeded had he not made mistakes in other particulars of conduct.

By the recovery of Lombardy, Louis at once regained the credit which Charles had lost. Genoa made submission; the Florentines came to terms; the Marquis of Mantua, the Duke of Ferrara, the Bentivogli, the Countess of Forlì, the Lords of Faenza, Pesaro, Rimini, Camerino, and Piombino, the citizens of Lucca, Pisa, and Siena, all came forward offering their friendship.[9] The Venetians, who to obtain possession of a couple of towns in Lombardy had made the French King master of two-thirds of Italy, had now cause to repent the rash game they had played.

Let any one, therefore, consider how easily King Louis might have maintained his authority in Italy had he observed the rules which I have noted above, and secured and protected all those friends of his, who being weak, and fearful, some of the Church, some of the Venetians, were of necessity obliged to attach themselves to him, and with whose assistance, for they were many, he might readily have made himself safe against any other powerful State. But no sooner was he in Milan than he took a contrary course, in helping Pope Alexander to occupy Romagna; not perceiving that in seconding this enterprise he weakened himself by alienating friends and those who had thrown themselves into his arms while he strengthened the Church by adding great temporal power to the spiritual power which of itself confers so mighty an authority. Making this first mistake, he was forced to follow it up, until at last, in order to curb the ambition of Pope Alexander, and prevent him becoming master of Tuscany, he was obliged to come himself into Italy.[10]

And as though it were not enough for him to have aggrandized the Church and stripped himself of friends, he must needs in his desire to possess the Kingdom of Naples, divide it with the King of Spain,[11] thus bringing into Italy, where before he had been supreme, a rival to whom the ambitious and discontented in that Province might have recourse. And whereas he might have left in Naples a King willing to hold as his tributary, he displaced him to make way for another strong enough to effect his expulsion.[12] The wish to acquire is no doubt a natural and common sentiment, and when men attempt things within their power, they will always be praised rather than blamed. But when they persist in attempts that are beyond their power, mishaps and blame ensue. If France, therefore, with her own forces could have attacked Naples, she should have done so. If she could not, she ought not to have divided it. And if her partition of Lombardy with the Venetians may be excused as the means whereby a footing was gained in Italy, this other partition is to be condemned as not justified by the like necessity.

Louis, then, had made these five blunders. He had destroyed weaker States, he had strengthened a Prince already strong, he had brought into the country a very powerful stranger, he had not come to reside, and he had not sent colonies. And yet all these blunders might not have proved disastrous to him while he lived, had he not added to them a sixth in depriving the Venetians of their dominions.[13] For had he neither aggrandized the Church, nor brought Spain into Italy, it might have been at once reasonable and necessary to humble the Venetians; but after committing himself to these other courses, he should never have consented to the ruin of

Venice. For while the Venetians were powerful they would always have kept others back from an attempt on Lombardy, as well because they never would have agreed to that enterprise on any terms save of themselves being made its masters, as because others would never have desired to take it from France in order to hand it over to them, nor would ever have ventured to defy both. And if it be said that King Louis ceded Romagna to Alexander, and Naples to Spain in order to avoid war, I answer that for the reasons already given, you ought never to suffer your designs to be crossed in order to avoid war, since war is not so to be avoided, but is only deferred to your disadvantage. And if others should allege the King's promise to the Pope to undertake that enterprise on his behalf,[14] in return for the dissolution of his marriage, and for the Cardinal's hat conferred on d'Amboise, I answer by referring to what I say further on concerning the faith of Princes and how it is to be kept.

King Louis, therefore, lost Lombardy from not following any one of the methods pursued by others who have taken Provinces with the resolve to keep them. Nor is this anything strange, but only what might reasonably and naturally be looked for. And on this very subject I spoke to d'Amboise at Nantes, at the time when Duke Valentino, as Cesare Borgia, son to Pope Alexander, was vulgarly called, was occupying Romagna.[15] For, on the Cardinal saying to me that the Italians did not understand war, I answered that the French did not understand statecraft, for had they done so, they never would have allowed the Church to grow so powerful. And the event shows that the aggrandizement of the Church and of Spain in Italy has been brought about by France, and that the ruin of France has been wrought by them. Whence we may draw the general axiom, which never or rarely errs, that *he who is the cause of another's greatness is himself undone,* since he must work either by address or force, each of which excites distrust in the person raised to power.

Chapter IV

WHY THE KINGDOM OF DARIUS, CONQUERED BY ALEXANDER, DID NOT, ON ALEXANDER'S DEATH, REBEL AGAINST HIS SUCCESSORS

ALEXANDER THE GREAT having achieved the conquest of Asia in a few years, and dying before he had well entered on possession, it might have been expected, having regard to the difficulty of preserving newly acquired States, that on his death the whole country would rise in revolt. Nevertheless, his successors were able to keep their hold, and found in doing so no other difficulty than arose from their own ambition and mutual jealousies.[1]

If any one think this strange and ask the cause, I answer, that all the Princedoms of which we have record have been governed in one or other of two ways, either by a sole Prince, all others being his servants permitted by his grace and favour to assist in governing the kingdom as his ministers; or else, by a Prince with his Barons who hold their rank, not by the favour of a superior Lord, but by antiquity of blood, and who have States and subjects of their own who recognize them as their rulers and entertain for them a natural affection.

States governed by a sole Prince and by his servants vest in him a more complete authority; because throughout the land none but he is recognized as sovereign, and if obedience be yielded to any others, it is yielded as to his ministers and officers for whom personally no special love is felt.

Of these two forms of government we have examples in our own days in the Turk and the King of France. The whole Turkish empire is governed by a sole Prince, all others being his slaves. Dividing his kingdom into *sandjaks,* he sends thither different governors whom he shifts and changes at his pleasure.[2] The King of France, on the other hand, is surrounded by a multitude of nobles of ancient descent, each acknowledged and loved by subjects of his own, and each asserting a precedence in rank of which the King can deprive him only at his peril.

He, therefore, who considers the different character of these two States, will perceive that it would be difficult to gain possession of that of the Turk, but that once won it might be easily held. The obstacles to its conquest are that the invader cannot be called in by a native nobility, nor expect his enterprise to be aided by the defection of those whom the sovereign has around him. And this for the various reasons already given, namely, that all being slaves and under obligations they are not easily corrupted, or if corrupted can render little assistance, being unable, as I have already explained, to carry the people with them. Whoever, therefore, attacks the Turk must reckon on finding a united people, and must trust rather to his own strength than to divisions on the other side. But were his adversary once overcome and defeated in the field, so that he could not repair his armies, no cause for anxiety would remain, except in the family of the Prince; which being extirpated, there would be none else to fear; for since all beside are without credit with the people, the invader, as before his victory he had nothing to hope from them, so after it has nothing to dread.

But the contrary is the case in kingdoms governed like that of France, into which, because men who are discontented and desirous of change are always to be found, you may readily procure an entrance by gaining over some Baron of the Realm.[3] Such persons, for the reasons already given, are able to open the way to you for the invasion of their country and to render its conquest easy. But afterwards the effort to hold your ground involves you in endless difficulties, as well in respect of those who have helped you, as of those whom you have overthrown. Nor will it be enough to have destroyed the family of the Prince, since all those other Lords remain to put themselves at the head of new movements; whom being unable either to content or to destroy, you lose the State whenever occasion serves them.

Now, if you examine the nature of the government of Darius, you will find that it resembled that of the Turk, and, consequently, that it was necessary for Alexander, first of all, to defeat him utterly and strip him of his dominions; after which defeat, Darius having died, the country, for the causes above explained, was permanently secured to Alexander. And had his successors continued united they might have enjoyed it undisturbed, since there arose no disorders in that kingdom save those of their own creating.

But kingdoms ordered like that of France cannot be

retained with the same ease. Hence the repeated risings of Spain, Gaul, and Greece against the Romans, resulting from the number of small Princedoms of which these Provinces were made up. For while the memory of these lasted, the Romans could never think their tenure safe. But when that memory was worn out by the authority and long continuance of their rule, they gained a secure hold, and were able afterwards in their contests among themselves, each to carry with him some portion of these Provinces, according as each had acquired influence there; for these, on the extinction of the line of their old Princes, came to recognize no other Lords than the Romans.

Bearing all this in mind, no one need wonder at the ease wherewith Alexander was able to lay a firm hold on Asia, nor that Pyrrhus[4] and many others found difficulty in preserving other acquisitions; since this arose, not from the less or greater merit of the conquerors, but from the different character of the States with which they had to deal.

Chapter V

How Cities or Provinces Which before Their Acquisition Have Lived under Their Own Laws Are to Be Governed

WHEN A NEWLY acquired State has been accustomed, as I have said, to live under its own laws and in freedom, there are three methods whereby it may be held. The first is to destroy it; the second, to go and reside there in person; the third, to suffer it to live on under its own laws, subjecting it to a tribute, and entrusting its government to a few of the inhabitants who will keep the rest your friends. Such a Government, since it is the creature of the new Prince, will see that it cannot stand without his protection and support, and must therefore do all it can to maintain him; and a city accustomed to live in freedom, if it is to be preserved at all, is more easily controlled through its own citizens than in any other way.

We have examples of all these methods in the histories of the Spartans and the Romans. The Spartans held Athens and Thebes by creating oligarchies in these cities, yet lost them in the end.[1] The Romans, to retain Capua, Carthage, and Numantia, destroyed them and never lost them.[2] On the other hand, when they thought to hold Greece as the Spartans had held it, leaving it its freedom and allowing it to be governed by its own laws, they failed, and had to destroy many cities of that Province before they could secure it. For, in truth, there is no sure way of holding other than by destroying, and whoever becomes master of a City accustomed to live in freedom and does not destroy it, may reckon on being destroyed by it. For if it should rebel, it can always screen itself under the name of liberty and its ancient laws, which no length of time, nor any benefits conferred will ever cause it to forget; and do what you will, and take what care you may, unless the inhabitants be scattered and dispersed, this name, and the old order of things, will never cease to be remembered, but will at once be turned against you whenever misfortune overtakes you, as when Pisa rose against the Florentines after a hundred years of servitude.[3]

If, however, the newly acquired City or Province has been accustomed to live under a Prince, and his line is extinguished, it will be impossible for the citizens, used, on the one hand, to obey, and deprived, on the other, of their old ruler, to agree to choose a leader from among themselves; and as they know not how to live as freemen, and are therefore slow to take up arms, a stranger may readily gain them over and attach them to his cause. But in Republics there is a stronger vitality, a fiercer hatred, a keener thirst for revenge. The memory of their former freedom will not let them rest; so that the safest course is either to destroy them, or to go and live in them.

Chapter VI

OF NEW PRINCEDOMS WHICH A PRINCE ACQUIRES WITH HIS OWN ARMS AND BY MERIT

LET NO MAN marvel if in what I am about to say concerning Princedoms wholly new, both as regards the Prince and the form of Government, I cite the highest examples. For since men for the most part follow in the footsteps and imitate the actions of others, and yet are unable to adhere exactly to those paths which others have taken, or attain to the virtues of those whom they would resemble, the wise man should always follow the roads that have been trodden by the great, and imitate those who have most excelled, so that if he cannot reach their perfection, he may at least acquire something of its savour. Acting in this like the skilful archer, who seeing that the object he would hit is distant, and knowing the range of his bow, takes aim much above the destined mark; not designing that his arrow should strike so high, but that flying high it may alight at the point intended.

I say, then, that in entirely new Princedoms where the Prince himself is new, the difficulty of maintaining possession varies with the greater or less ability of him who acquires possession. And, because the mere fact of a private person rising to be a Prince presupposes either merit or good fortune, it will be seen that the presence of one or other of these two conditions lessens, to some extent, many difficulties. And yet, he who is less beholden to Fortune has often in the end the better success; and it may be for the advantage of a Prince that, from his having no other territories, he is obliged to reside in person in the State which he has acquired.

Looking first to those who have become Princes by their merit and not by their good fortune, I say that the most excellent among them are Moses, Cyrus, Romulus, Theseus, and the like.[1] And though perhaps I ought not to name Moses, he being merely an instrument for carrying out the Divine commands, he is still to be admired for those qualities which made him worthy to converse with God. But if we consider Cyrus and the others who have acquired or founded kingdoms, they will all be seen to be admirable. And if their actions and the particular institutions of which they were the authors be studied, they will be found not to differ from those of Moses, instructed though he was by so great a teacher. Moreover, on examining their lives and actions, we shall see that they were debtors to Fortune for nothing beyond the opportunity which enabled them to shape things as they pleased, without which the force of their spirit would have been spent in vain; as on the other hand, opportunity would have offered itself in vain, had the capacity for turning it to account been wanting. It was necessary, therefore, that Moses should find the children of Israel in bondage in Egypt, and oppressed by the Egyptians, in order that they might be disposed to follow him, and so escape from their servitude. It was fortunate for Romulus that he found no home in Alba, but was exposed at the time of his birth, to the end that he might become king and founder of the City of Rome. It was necessary that Cyrus should find the Persians discontented with the rule of the Medes, and the Medes enervated and effeminate from a prolonged peace. Nor could Theseus have displayed his great qualities had he not found the Athenians disunited and dispersed. But while it was their opportunities that made these men fortunate, it was their own merit that enabled them to recognize these opportunities and turn them to account, to the glory and prosperity of their country.

They who come to the Princedom, as these did, by virtuous paths, acquire with difficulty, but keep with ease. The difficulties which they have in acquiring arise mainly from the new laws and institutions which they are forced to introduce in founding and securing their government. And let it be noted that there is no more delicate matter to take in hand, nor more dangerous to conduct, nor more doubtful in its success, than to set up as a leader in the introduction of changes. For he who innovates will have for his enemies all those who are well off under the existing order of things, and only lukewarm supporters in those who might be better off under the new. This lukewarm temper arises partly from the fear of adversaries who have the laws on their side, and partly from the incredulity of mankind, who will never admit the merit of anything new, until they have seen it proved by the event. The result, however, is that whenever the enemies of change make an attack, they do so with all the zeal of partisans, while the others defend themselves so feebly as to endanger both themselves and their cause.

But to get a clearer understanding of this part of our subject, we must look whether these innovators can stand alone, or whether they depend for aid upon others; in other words, whether to carry out their ends they must resort to entreaty, or can prevail by force. In the former case they always fare badly and bring nothing to a successful issue; but when they depend upon their own resources and can employ force, they seldom fail. Hence it comes that all armed Prophets have been victorious, and all unarmed Prophets have been destroyed.

For, besides what has been said, it should be borne in mind that the temper of the multitude is fickle, and that while it is easy to persuade them of a thing, it is hard to fix them in that persuasion. Wherefore, matters should be so ordered that when men no longer believe of their own accord, they may be compelled to believe by force. Moses, Cyrus, Theseus, and Romulus could never have made their ordinances be observed for any length of time had they been unarmed, as was the case, in our own days, with the Friar Girolamo Savonarola, whose new institutions came to nothing so soon as the multitude began to waver in their faith; since he had not the means to keep those who had been believers steadfast in their belief, or to make unbelievers believe.[2]

Such persons, therefore, have great difficulty in carrying out their designs; but all their difficulties are on the road, and may be overcome by courage. Having conquered these, and coming to be held in reverence, and having destroyed all who were jealous of their influence, they remain powerful, safe, honoured, and prosperous.

To the great examples cited above, I would add one other, of less note indeed, but assuredly bearing some proportion to them, and which may stand for all others of a like character. I mean the example of Hiero the Syracusan. He from a private station rose to be Prince of Syracuse,[3] and he too was indebted to Fortune only for his opportunity. For the Syracusans being oppressed, chose him to be their Captain, which office he so discharged as deservedly to be made their King. For even while a private citizen his merit was so remarkable, that one who writes of him says, he lacked nothing that a King should have save the Kingdom. Doing away with the old army, he organized a new, abandoned existing alliances and assumed new allies, and with an army and allies of his own, was able on that foundation to build what superstructure he pleased; having trouble enough in acquiring, but none in preserving what he had acquired.

Chapter VII

OF NEW PRINCEDOMS ACQUIRED BY THE AID OF OTHERS AND BY GOOD FORTUNE

THEY WHO from a private station become Princes by mere good fortune, do so with little trouble, but have much trouble to maintain themselves. They meet with no hindrance on their way, being carried as it were on wings to their destination, but all their difficulties overtake them when they alight. Of this class are those on whom States are conferred either in return for money, or through the favour of him who confers them; as it happened to many in the Greek cities of Ionia and the Hellespont to be made Princes by Darius,[1] that they might hold these cities for his security and glory; and as happened in the case of those Emperors who, from privacy, attained the Imperial dignity by corrupting the army. Such Princes are wholly dependent on the favour and fortunes of those who have made them great, than which supports none could be less stable or secure; and they lack both the knowledge and the power that would enable them to maintain their position. They lack the knowledge, because unless they have great parts and force of character, it is not to be expected that having always lived in a private station they should have learned how to command. They lack the power, since they cannot look for support from attached and faithful troops. Moreover, States suddenly acquired, like all else that is produced and that grows up rapidly, can never have such root or hold as that the first storm which strikes them shall not overthrow them; unless, indeed, as I have said already, they who thus suddenly become Princes have a capacity for learning quickly how to defend what Fortune has placed in their lap, and can lay those foundations after they rise which by others are laid before.

Of each of these methods of becoming a Prince, namely, by merit and by good fortune, I shall select an instance from times within my own recollection, and shall take the cases of Francesco Sforza and Cesare Borgia. By suitable measures and singular ability, Francesco Sforza rose from privacy to be Duke of Milan, preserving with little trouble what it cost him infinite efforts to gain. On the other hand, Cesare Borgia, vulgarly spoken of as Duke Valentino, obtained his Princedom through the favourable fortunes of his father, and with these lost it, although, so far as in him lay, he used every effort and practised every expedient that a prudent and able man should, who desires to strike root in a State given him by the arms and fortune of another. For, as I have already said, he who does not lay his foundations at first, may, if he be of great parts, succeed in laying them afterwards, though with inconvenience to the builder and risk to the building. And if we consider the various measures taken by Duke Valentino, we shall perceive how broad were the foundations he had laid whereon to rest his future power.

These I think it not superfluous to examine, since I know not what lessons I could teach a new Prince, more useful than the example of his actions. And if the measures taken by him did not profit him in the end, it was through no fault of his, but from the extraordinary and extreme malignity of Fortune.

In his efforts to aggrandize the Duke his son, Alexander VI had to face many difficulties, both immediate and remote. In the first place, he saw no way to make him Lord of any State which was not a State of the Church, while, if he sought to take for him a State belonging to the Church, he knew that the Duke of Milan and the Venetians would withhold their consent; Faenza and Rimini being already under the protection of the latter. Further, he saw that the arms of Italy, and those more especially of which he might have availed himself, were in the hands of men who had reason to fear his aggrandizement, that is, of the Orsini, the Colonnesi,[2] and their followers. These therefore he could not trust. It was consequently necessary that the existing order of things should be changed, and the States of Italy thrown into confusion, in order that he might safely make himself master of some part of them; and this became easy for him when he found that the Venetians, moved by other causes, were plotting to bring the French once more into Italy. This design he accordingly did not oppose, but furthered by annulling the first marriage of the French King.[3]

King Louis therefore came into Italy at the instance of the Venetians, and with the consent of Pope Alexander, and no sooner was he in Milan than the Pope got

troops from him to aid him in his enterprise against Romagna,[4] which Province, moved by the reputation of
the French arms, at once submitted. After thus obtaining possession of Romagna, and after quelling the
Colonnesi, Duke Valentino was desirous to follow up
and extend his conquests. Two causes, however, held
him back, namely, the doubtful fidelity of his own
forces, and the waywardness of France. For he feared
that the Orsini, of whose arms he had made use, might
fail him, and not merely prove a hindrance to further
acquisitions, but take from him what he had gained, and
that the King might serve him the same turn. How little
he could count on the Orsini was made plain when,
after the capture of Faenza, he turned his arms against
Bologna; and saw how reluctantly they took part in that
enterprise. The King's mind he understood, when, after
seizing on the Dukedom of Urbino, he was about to attack Tuscany; from which design Louis compelled him
to desist.[5] Whereupon the Duke resolved to depend no
longer on the arms or fortune of others. His first step,
therefore, was to weaken the factions of the Orsini and
Colonnesi in Rome. Those of their following who were
of good birth, he gained over by making them his own
gentlemen, assigning them a liberal provision, and con-
ferring upon them commands and appointments suited
to their rank; so that in a few months their old partisan
attachments died out, and the hopes of all rested on the
Duke alone.

He then awaited an occasion to crush the chiefs of
the Orsini, for those of the house of Colonna he had already scattered, and a good opportunity presenting itself, he turned it to the best account. For when the
Orsini came at last to see that the greatness of the Duke

and the Church involved their ruin, they assembled a council at Magione in the Perugian territory, whence resulted the revolt of Urbino, commotions in Romagna, and an infinity of dangers to the Duke, all of which he overcame with the help of France. His credit thus restored, the Duke trusting no longer either to the French or to any other foreign aid, that he might not have to confront them openly, resorted to stratagem, and was so well able to dissemble his designs, that the Orsini, through the mediation of Signor Paolo[6] (whom he failed not to secure by every friendly attention, furnishing him with clothes, money, and horses), were so won over as to be drawn in their simplicity into his hands at Sinigaglia.[7] When the leaders were thus disposed of, and their followers made his friends, the Duke had laid sufficiently good foundations for his future power, since he held all Romagna together with the Dukedom of Urbino, and had ingratiated himself with the entire population of these States, who now began to see that they were well off.

And since this part of his conduct merits both attention and imitation, I shall not pass it over in silence. After the Duke had taken Romagna, finding that it had been ruled by feeble Lords, who thought more of plundering than correcting their subjects, and gave them more cause for division than for union, so that the country was overrun with robbery, tumult, and every kind of outrage, he judged it necessary, with a view to render it peaceful and obedient to his authority, to provide it with a good government. Accordingly he set over it Messer Remiro d'Orco, a stern and prompt ruler, who being entrusted with the fullest powers, in a very short time, and with much credit to himself, restored it to tranquillity and order. But afterwards apprehending that such unlimited authority might become odious, the Duke decided that it was no longer needed, and established in the centre of the Province a civil Tribunal, with an excellent President, in which every town was represented by its advocate. And knowing that past severities had generated ill-feeling against himself, in order to purge the minds of the people and gain their good-will, he sought to show them that any cruelty which had been done had not originated with him, but in the harsh disposition of his minister. Availing himself of the pretext which this afforded, he one morning caused Remiro to be beheaded, and exposed in the market place of Cesena with a block and bloody axe by his side. The barbarity of which spectacle at once astounded and satisfied the populace.[8]

But, returning to the point whence we diverged, I say that the Duke, finding himself fairly strong and in a measure secured against present dangers, being furnished with arms of his own choosing and having to a great extent got rid of those which, if left near him, might have caused him trouble, had to consider, if he desired to follow up his conquests, how he was to deal with France, since he saw he could expect no further support from King Louis, whose eyes were at last opened to his mistake. He therefore began to look about for new alliances, and to waver in his adherence to the French, then occupied with their expedition into the kingdom of Naples against the Spaniards, at that time laying siege to Gaeta; his object being to secure himself against France; and in this he would soon have succeeded had Alexander lived.[9]

Such was the line he took to meet present exigencies.

As regards the future, he had to apprehend that a new Head of the Church might not be his friend, and might even seek to deprive him of what Alexander had given. This he thought to provide against in four ways. First, by exterminating all who were of kin to those Lords whom he had despoiled of their possessions, that they might not become instruments in the hands of a new Pope. Second, by gaining over all the Roman nobles, so as to be able with their help to put a bridle, as the saying is, in the Pope's mouth. Third, by bringing the College of Cardinals, so far as he could, under his control. And fourth, by establishing his authority so firmly before his father's death, as to be able by himself to withstand the shock of a first onset.

Of these measures, at the time when Alexander died, he had already effected three, and had almost carried out the fourth. For of the Lords whose possessions he had usurped, he had put to death all whom he could reach, and very few had escaped. He had gained over the Roman nobility, and had the majority in the College of Cardinals on his side.

As to further acquisitions, his design was to make himself master of Tuscany. He was already in possession of Perugia and Piombino, and had assumed the protectorship of Pisa,[10] on which city he was about to spring; taking no heed of France, as indeed he no longer had occasion, since the French had been deprived of the kingdom of Naples by the Spaniards under circumstances which made it necessary for both nations to buy his friendship. Pisa taken, Lucca and Siena would soon have yielded, partly through jealousy of Florence, partly through fear, and the position of the Florentines must then have been desperate.

Had he therefore succeeded in these designs, as he was succeeding in that very year in which Alexander died, he would have won such power and reputation that he might afterwards have stood alone, relying on his own strength and resources, without being beholden to the power and fortune of others. But Alexander died five years from the time he first unsheathed the sword, leaving his son with the State of Romagna alone consolidated, with all the rest unsettled, between two powerful hostile armies, and sick almost to death. And yet such were the fire and courage of the Duke, he knew so well how men must either be conciliated or crushed, and so solid were the foundations he had laid in that brief period, that had these armies not been upon his back, or had he been in sound health, he must have surmounted every difficulty.

How strong his foundations were may be seen from this, that Romagna waited for him for more than a month; and that although half dead, he remained in safety in Rome, where though the Baglioni, the Vitelli, and the Orsini came to attack him, they met with no success. Moreover, since he was able if not to make whom he liked Pope, at least to prevent the election of any whom he disliked,[11] had he been in health at the time when Alexander died, all would have been easy for him. But he told me himself on the day on which Julius II was created, that he had foreseen and provided for everything else that could happen on his father's death, but had never anticipated that when his father died he too should be at death's door.

Taking all these actions of the Duke together, I can find no fault with him; nay, it seems to me reasonable to put him forward, as I have done, as a pattern for all such as rise to power by good fortune and the help of others. For with his great spirit and high aims he could not act otherwise than he did, and nothing but the shortness of his father's life and his own illness prevented the success of his designs. Whoever, therefore, on entering a new Princedom, judges it necessary to rid himself of enemies, to conciliate friends, to prevail by force or fraud, to make himself feared yet not hated by his subjects, respected and obeyed by his soldiers, to crush those who can or ought to injure him, to introduce changes in the old order of things, to be at once severe and affable, magnanimous and liberal, to do away with a mutinous army and create a new one, to maintain relations with Kings and Princes on such a footing that they must see it for their interest to aid him, and dangerous to offend, can find no brighter example than in the actions of this Prince.

The one thing for which he may be blamed was the creation of Pope Julius II, in respect of whom he chose badly. Because, as I have said already, though he could not secure the election he desired, he could have prevented any other; and he ought never to have consented to the creation of any one of those Cardinals whom he had injured, or who on becoming Pope would have reason to fear him; for fear is as dangerous an enemy as resentment. Those whom he had offended were, among others, San Pietro ad Vincula, Colonna, San Giorgio, and Ascanio; all the rest, excepting d'Amboise and the Spanish Cardinals (the latter from their connexion and obligations, the former from the power he derived through his relations with the French Court), would on assuming the Pontificate have had reason to fear him. The Duke, therefore, ought, in the first place, to have laboured for the creation of a Spanish Pope; failing in which, he should have agreed to the election of d'Amboise, but never to that of San Pietro ad Vincula. And he deceives himself who believes that with the great, recent benefits cause old wrongs to be forgotten.

The Duke, therefore, erred in the part he took in this election; and his error was the cause of his ultimate downfall.

Chapter VIII

OF THOSE WHO BY THEIR CRIMES COME TO BE PRINCES

BUT SINCE from privacy a man may also rise to be a Prince in one or other of two ways, neither of which can be referred wholly either to merit or to fortune, it is fit that I notice them here, though one of them may fall to be discussed more fully in treating of Republics.

The ways I speak of are, first, when the ascent to power is made by paths of wickedness and crime; and second, when a private person becomes ruler of his country by the favour of his fellow-citizens. The former method I shall make clear by two examples, one ancient, the other modern, without entering further into the merits of the matter, for these, I think, should be enough for any one who is driven to follow them.

Agathocles the Sicilian came, not merely from a private station, but from the very dregs of the people, to be King of Syracuse.[1] Son of a potter, through all the stages of his fortunes he led a foul life. His vices, however, were conjoined with so great vigour both of mind and body, that becoming a soldier, he rose through the various grades of the service to be Praetor of Syracuse. Once established in that post, he resolved to make himself Prince, and to hold by violence and without obligation to others the authority which had been spontaneously entrusted to him. Accordingly, after imparting his design to Hamilcar, who with the Carthaginian armies was at that time waging war in Sicily, he one morning assembled the people and senate of Syracuse as though to consult with them on matters of public moment, and on a preconcerted signal caused his soldiers to put to death all the senators, and the wealthiest of the commons. These being thus got rid of, he assumed and retained possession of the sovereignty without opposition on the part of the people; and although twice defeated by the Carthaginians, and afterwards besieged, he was able not only to defend his city, but leaving a part of his forces for its protection, to invade Africa with the remainder, and so in a short time to raise the siege of Syracuse, reducing the Carthaginians to the utmost extremities, and compelling them to make terms whereby they abandoned Sicily to him and confined themselves to Africa.

Whoever examines this man's actions and achievements will discover little or nothing in them which can be ascribed to Fortune, seeing, as has already been said, that it was not through the favour of any, but by the regular steps of the military service, gained at the cost of a thousand hardships and hazards, he reached the princedom which he afterwards maintained by so many daring and dangerous enterprises. Still, to slaughter fellow-citizens, to betray friends, to be devoid of honour, pity, and religion, cannot be counted as merits, for these are means which may lead to power, but which confer no glory. Wherefore, if in respect of the valour with which he encountered and extricated himself from difficulties, and the constancy of his spirit in supporting and conquering adverse fortune, there seems no reason to judge him inferior to the greatest captains that have ever lived, his unbridled cruelty and inhumanity, together with his countless crimes, forbid us to number him with the greatest men; but, at any rate, we cannot attribute to Fortune or to merit what he accomplished without either.

In our own times, during the papacy of Alexander VI, Oliverotto of Fermo, who some years before had been left an orphan, and had been brought up by his maternal uncle Giovanni Fogliani, was sent while still a lad to serve under Paolo Vitelli, in the expectation that a thorough training under that commander might qualify him for high rank as a soldier. After the death of Paolo, he served under his brother Vitellozzo, and in a very short time, being of a quick wit, hardy and resolute, he became one of the first soldiers of his company. But thinking it beneath him to serve under others, with the countenance of the Vitelleschi and the connivance of certain citizens of Fermo who preferred the slavery to the freedom of their country, he formed the design to seize on that town.

He accordingly wrote to Giovanni Fogliani that after many years of absence from home, he desired to see him and his native city once more, and to look a little into the condition of his patrimony; and as his one endeavour had been to make himself a name, in order that his fellow-citizens might see that his time had not been mis-spent, he proposed to return honourably attended by a hundred horsemen from among his own friends and followers; and he begged Giovanni graciously to arrange for his reception by the citizens of Fermo with corresponding marks of distinction, as this would be creditable not only to himself, but also to the uncle who had brought him up.

Giovanni accordingly did not fail in any proper attention to his nephew, but caused him to be splendidly received by his fellow-citizens, and lodged him in his house; where Oliverotto having passed some days, and made the necessary arrangements for carrying out his wickedness, gave a formal banquet, to which he invited his uncle and all the first men of Fermo. When the repast and the other entertainments proper to such an occasion had come to an end, Oliverotto artfully turned the conversation to matters of grave interest, by speaking of the greatness of Pope Alexander and Cesare his son, and of their enterprises; and when Giovanni and the others were replying to what he said, he suddenly rose up, observing that these were matters to be discussed in a more private place, and so withdrew to another chamber; whither his uncle and all the other citizens followed him, and where they had no sooner seated themselves, than soldiers rushing out from places of concealment put Giovanni and all the rest to death.

After this butchery, Oliverotto mounted his horse, rode through the streets, and besieged the chief magistrate in the palace, so that all were constrained by fear to yield obedience and accept a government of which he made himself the head. And all who from being disaffected were likely to stand in his way, he put to death, while he strengthened himself with new ordinances, civil and military, to such purpose, that for the space of a year during which he retained the Princedom, he not merely kept a firm hold of the city, but grew formidable to all his neighbours. And it would have been as impossible to unseat him as it was to unseat Agathocles, had he not let himself be overreached by Cesare Borgia on the occasion when, as has already been told, the Orsini and Vitelli were entrapped at Sinigaglia; where he too being taken, one year after the commission of his parricidal crime, was strangled along with Vitellozzo, whom he had assumed for his master in villainy as in valour.

It may be asked how Agathocles and some like him, after numberless acts of treachery and cruelty, have been able to live long in their own country in safety, and to defend themselves from foreign enemies, without being plotted against by their fellow-citizens, whereas, many others, by reason of their cruelty, have failed to maintain their position even in peaceful times, not to speak of the perilous times of war. I believe that this results from cruelty being well or ill employed. Those cruelties we may say are well employed, if it be permitted to speak well of things evil, which are done once for all under the necessity of self-preservation, and are not afterwards persisted in, but so far as possible modified to the advantage of the governed. Ill-employed cruelties, on the other hand, are those which from small beginnings increase rather than diminish with time. They who follow the first of these methods, may, by the grace of God and man, find, as did Agathocles, that their condition is not desperate; but by no possibility can the others maintain themselves.

Hence we may learn the lesson that on seizing a state, the usurper should make haste to inflict what injuries he must, at a stroke, that he may not have to renew them daily, but be enabled by their discontinuance to reassure men's minds, and afterwards win them over by benefits. Whosoever, either through timidity or from following bad counsels, adopts a contrary course, must keep the sword always drawn, and can put no trust in his subjects, who suffering from continued and constantly renewed severities, will never yield him their confidence. Injuries, therefore, should be inflicted all at once, that their ill savour being less lasting may the less offend; whereas, benefits should be conferred little by little, that so they may be more fully relished.

But, before all things, a Prince should so live with his subjects that no vicissitude of good or evil fortune shall oblige him to alter his behaviour; because, if a need to change come through adversity, it is then too late to resort to severity; while any leniency you may use will be thrown away, for it will be seen to be compulsory and gain you no thanks.

Chapter IX

OF THE CIVIL PRINCEDOM

I COME now to the second case, namely, of the leading citizen who, not by crimes or violence, but by the favour of his fellow-citizens is made Prince of his country. This may be called a Civil Princedom, and its attainment depends not wholly on merit, nor wholly on good fortune, but rather on what may be termed a *fortunate astuteness*. I say then that the road to this Princedom lies either through the favour of the people or of the nobles. For in every city are to be found these two opposed humours having their origin in this, that the people desire not to be domineered over or oppressed by the nobles, while the nobles desire to oppress and domineer over the people. And from these two contrary appetites there arises in cities one of three results, a Princedom, or Liberty, or Licence. A Princedom is created either by the people or by the nobles, according as one or other of these factions has occasion for it. For when the nobles perceive that they cannot withstand the people, they set to work to magnify the reputation of one of their number, and make him their Prince, to the end that under his shadow they may be enabled to indulge their desires. The people, on the other hand, when they see that they cannot make head against the nobles, invest a single citizen with all their influence and make him Prince, that they may have the shelter of his authority.

He who is made Prince by the favour of the nobles, has greater difficulty to maintain himself than he who comes to the Princedom by aid of the people, since he finds many about him who think themselves as good as he, and whom, on that account, he cannot guide or govern as he would. But he who reaches the Princedom by the popular support, finds himself alone, with none, or but a very few about him who are not ready to obey. Moreover, the demands of the nobles cannot be satisfied with credit to the Prince, nor without injury to others, while those of the people well may, the aim of the people being more honourable than that of the nobles, the latter seeking to oppress, the former not to be oppressed. Add to this, that a Prince can never secure himself against a disaffected people, their number being too great, while he may against a disaffected nobility, since their number is small. The worst that a Prince need fear from a disaffected people is, that they may desert him, whereas when the nobles are his enemies he has to fear not only that they may desert him, but also that they may turn against him; because, as they have greater craft and foresight, they always choose their time to suit their safety, and seek favour with the side they think will win. Again, a Prince must always live with the same people, but need not always live with the same nobles, being able to make and unmake these from day to day, and give and take away their authority at his pleasure.

But to make this part of the matter clearer, I say that as regards the nobles there is this first distinction to be made. They either so govern their conduct as to bind themselves wholly to your fortunes, or they do not. Those who so bind themselves, and who are not grasping, should be loved and honoured. As to those who do not so bind themselves, there is this further distinction. For the most part they are held back by pusillanimity and a natural defect of courage, in which case you should make use of them, and of those among them more especially who are prudent, for they will do you honour in prosperity, and in adversity give you no cause for fear. But where they abstain from attaching themselves to you of set purpose and for ambitious ends, it is a sign that they are thinking more of themselves than of you, and against such men a Prince should be on his guard, and treat them as though they were declared enemies, for in his adversity they will always help to ruin him.

He who becomes a Prince through the favour of the people should always keep on good terms with them; which it is easy for him to do, since all they ask is not to be oppressed. But he who against the will of the people is made a Prince by the favour of the nobles, must, above all things, seek to conciliate the people, which he readily may by taking them under his protection. For since men who are well treated by one whom they expected to treat them ill, feel the more beholden to their benefactor, the people will at once become better disposed to such a Prince when he protects them, than if he owed his Princedom to them.

There are many ways in which a Prince may gain the good will of the people, but, because these vary with circumstances, no certain rule can be laid down respecting them, and I shall, therefore, say no more about them. But this is the sum of the matter, that it is essential for a Prince to be on a friendly footing with his people, since, otherwise, he will have no resource in adversity. Nabis, Prince of Sparta, was attacked by the whole hosts of Greece, and by a Roman army flushed with victory, and defended his country and crown against them; and when danger approached, there were but few of his subjects against whom he needed to guard himself, whereas had the people been hostile, this would not have been enough.

And what I affirm let no one controvert by citing the old saw that *he who builds on the people builds on mire*, for that may be true of a private citizen who presumes on his favour with the people, and counts on being rescued by them when overpowered by his enemies or by the magistrates. In such cases a man may often find himself deceived, as happened to the Gracchi in Rome, and in Florence to Messer Giorgio Scali.[1] But when he who builds on the people is a Prince capable of command, of a spirit not to be cast down by ill fortune, who, while he animates the whole community by his courage and bearing, neglects no prudent precaution, he will not find himself betrayed by the people, but will be seen to have laid his foundations well.

The most critical juncture for Princedoms of this kind, is at the moment when they are about to pass from the popular to the absolute form of government: and as these Princes exercise their authority either directly or through the agency of the magistrates, in the latter case their position is weaker and more hazardous, since they are wholly in the power of those citizens to whom the magistracies are entrusted, who can, and especially in difficult times, with the greatest ease deprive them of their authority, either by opposing, or by not obeying them. And in times of peril it is too late for a Prince to assume to himself an absolute authority, for the citizens and subjects who are accustomed to take their orders from the magistrates, will not when dangers threaten take them from the Prince, so that at such seasons there will always be very few in whom he can trust. Such Princes, therefore, must not build on what they see in tranquil times when the citizens feel the need of the State. For then every one is ready to run, to promise, and, danger of death being remote, even to die for the State. But in troubled times, when the State has need of its citizens, few of them are to be found. And the risk of the experiment is the greater in that it can only be made once. Wherefore, a wise Prince should devise means whereby his subjects may at all times, whether favourable or adverse, feel the need of the State and of him, and then they will always be faithful to him.

Chapter X

How the Strength of All Princedoms Should Be Measured

$$\text{\Large ⚓}$$

IN EXAMINING the character of these Princedoms, another circumstance has to be considered, namely, whether the Prince is strong enough, if occasion demands, to stand alone, or whether he needs continual help from others. To make the matter clearer, I pronounce those to be able to stand alone who, with the men and money at their disposal, can get together an army fit to take the field against any assailant; and, conversely, I judge those to be in constant need of help who cannot take the field against their enemies, but are obliged to retire behind their walls, and to defend themselves there. Of the former I have already spoken, and shall speak again as occasion may require. As to the latter there is nothing to be said, except to exhort such Princes to strengthen and fortify the towns in which they dwell, and take no heed of the country outside. For whoever has thoroughly fortified his town, and put himself on such a footing with his subjects as I have already indicated and shall hereafter speak of, will always be attacked with much circumspection; for men are always averse to enterprises that are attended with difficulty, and it is impossible not to foresee difficulties in attacking a Prince whose town is strongly fortified and who is not hated by his subjects.

The towns of Germany enjoy great freedom. Having little territory, they render obedience to the Emperor only when so disposed, fearing neither him nor any other neighbouring power. For they are so fortified that it is plain to every one that it would be a tedious and difficult task to reduce them, since all of them are protected by moats and suitable ramparts, are well supplied with artillery, and keep their public magazines constantly stored with victual, drink and fuel, enough to last them for a year. Besides which, in order to support the poorer class of citizens without public loss, they lay in a common stock of materials for these to work on for a year, in the handicrafts which are the life and sinews of such cities, and by which the common people live. Moreover, they esteem military exercises and have many regulations for their maintenance.[1]

A Prince, therefore, who has a strong city, and who does not make himself hated, can not be attacked, or should he be so, his assailant will come badly off; since human affairs are so variable that it is almost impossible for any one to keep an army posted in leaguer for a whole year without interruption of some sort. Should it be objected that if the citizens have possessions outside the town, and see them burned, they will lose patience, and that self-interest, together with the hardships of a protracted siege, will cause them to forget their loyalty; I answer that a capable and courageous Prince will always overcome these difficulties, now, by holding out hopes to his subjects that the evil will not be of long continuance; now, by exciting their fears of the enemy's cruelty; and, again, by dexterously silencing those who seem to him too forward in their complaints. Moreover, it is to be expected that the enemy will burn and lay waste the country immediately on their arrival, at a time when men's minds are still heated and resolute for defence. And for this very reason the Prince ought the less to fear, because after a few days, when the first ardour has abated, the injury is already done and suffered, and cannot be undone; and the people will now, all the more readily, make common cause with their Prince from his seeming to be under obligations to them, their houses having been burned and their lands wasted in his defence. For it is the nature of men to incur obligation as much by the benefits they render as by those they receive.

Wherefore, if the whole matter be well considered, it ought not to be difficult for a prudent Prince, both at the outset and afterwards, to maintain the spirits of his subjects during a siege; provided always that victuals and the other means of defence do not run short.

Chapter XI

OF ECCLESIASTICAL PRINCEDOMS

IT NOW only remains for me to treat of Ecclesiastical Princedoms, all the difficulties in respect of which precede their acquisition. For they are acquired by merit or good fortune, but are maintained without either; being upheld by the venerable ordinances of Religion, which are all of such a nature and efficacy that they secure the authority of their Princes in whatever way they may act or live. These Princes alone have territories which they do not defend, and subjects whom they do not govern; yet their territories are not taken from them through not being defended, nor are their subjects concerned at not being governed, or led to think of throwing off their allegiance; nor is it in their power to do so. Accordingly these Princedoms alone are secure and happy. But inasmuch as they are sustained by agencies of a higher nature than the mind of man can reach, I forbear to speak of them: for since they are set up and supported by God himself, he would be a rash and presumptuous man who should venture to discuss them.

Nevertheless, should any one ask me how it comes about that the temporal power of the Church, which before the time of Alexander was looked on with contempt by all the Potentates of Italy, and not only by those so styling themselves, but by every Baron and Lordling however insignificant, has now reached such a pitch of greatness that the King of France trembles before it, and that it has been able to drive him out of Italy and to crush the Venetians;[1] though the causes be known, it seems to me not superfluous to call them in some measure to recollection.

Before Charles of France passed into Italy, that country was under the control of the Pope, the Venetians, the King of Naples, the Duke of Milan, and the Florentines. Two chief objects had to be kept in view by all these powers: first, that no armed foreigner should be allowed to invade Italy; second, that no one of their own number should be suffered to extend his territory. Those whom it was especially needed to guard against, were the Pope and the Venetians. To hold back the Venetians it was necessary that all the other States should combine, as was done for the defence of Ferrara; while to restrain the Pope, use was made of the Roman Barons, who being divided into two factions, the Orsini and Colonnesi, had constant cause for feud with one another, and standing with arms in their hands under the very eyes of the Pontiff, kept the Popedom feeble and insecure.

And although there arose from time to time a courageous Pope like Sixtus, neither his prudence nor his good fortune could free him from these embarrassments. The cause whereof was the shortness of the lives of the Popes. For in the ten years, which was the average duration of a Pope's life, he could barely succeed in humbling one of these factions; so that if, for instance, one Pope had almost exterminated the Colonnesi, he was followed by another, who being the enemy of the Orsini had no time to rid himself of them, but so far from completing the destruction of the Colonnesi, restored them to life. This led to the temporal authority of the Popes being little esteemed in Italy.

Then came Alexander VI, who more than any of his predecessors showed what a Pope could effect with money and arms, achieving by the instrumentality of Duke Valentino, and by taking advantage of the coming of the French into Italy, all those successes which I have already noticed in speaking of the actions of the Duke. And although his object was to aggrandize, not the Church but the Duke, what he did turned to the advantage of the Church, which after his death, and after the Duke had been put out of the way, became the heir of his labours.

After him came Pope Julius, who found the Church strengthened by the possession of the whole of Romagna, and the Roman Barons exhausted and their factions shattered under the blows of Pope Alexander. He found also a way opened for the accumulation of wealth, which before the time of Alexander no one had followed.[2] These advantages Julius not only used but added to. He undertook the conquest of Bologna, the overthrow of the Venetians, and the expulsion of the French from Italy; in all which enterprises he succeeded, and with the greater glory to himself in that whatever he did, was done to strengthen the Church and not to aggrandize any private person. He succeeded, moreover, in keeping the factions of the Orsini and Colonnesi within the same limits as he found them; and, though some seeds of insubordination may still have been left among them, two causes operated to hold them in check; first, the great power of the Church, which overawed them, and second, their being without Cardinals, who had been the cause of all their disorders. For these factions while they have Cardinals among them can never be at rest, since it is they who foment dissension both in Rome and out of it, in which the Barons are forced to take part, the ambition of the Prelates thus giving rise to tumult and discord among the Barons.

His Holiness, Pope Leo, has consequently found the Papacy most powerful; and from him we may hope, that as his predecessors made it great with arms, he will render it still greater and more venerable by his benignity and other countless virtues.

Chapter XII

HOW MANY DIFFERENT KINDS OF SOLDIERS THERE ARE, AND OF MERCENARIES

HAVING SPOKEN particularly of all the various kinds of Princedom whereof at the outset I proposed to treat, considered in some measure what are the causes of their strength and weakness, and pointed out the methods by which men commonly seek to acquire them, it now remains that I should discourse generally concerning the means for attack and defence of which each of these different kinds of Princedom may make use.

I have already said that a Prince must lay solid foundations, since otherwise he will inevitably be destroyed. Now the main foundations of all States, whether new, old, or mixed, are good laws and good arms. But since you cannot have the former without the latter, and where you have the latter, are likely to have the former, I shall here omit all discussion on the subject of laws, and speak only of arms.

I say then that the arms wherewith a Prince defends his State are either his own subjects, or they are mercenaries, or they are auxiliaries, or they are partly one and partly another. Mercenaries and auxiliaries are at once useless and dangerous, and he who holds his State by means of mercenary troops can never be solidly or securely seated. For such troops are disunited, ambitious, insubordinate, treacherous, insolent among friends, cowardly before foes, and without fear of God or faith with man. Whenever they are attacked defeat follows; so that in peace you are plundered by them, in war by your enemies. And this because they have no tie or motive to keep them in the field beyond their paltry pay, in return for which it would be too much to expect them to give their lives. They are ready enough, therefore, to be your soldiers while you are at peace, but when war is declared they make off and disappear. I ought to have little difficulty in getting this believed, for the present ruin of Italy is due to no other cause than her having for many years trusted to mercenaries, who though heretofore they may have helped the fortunes of some one man, and made a show of strength when matched with one another, have always revealed themselves in their true colours so soon as foreign enemies appeared. Hence it was that Charles of France was suffered to conquer Italy *with chalk;*[1] and he who said our sins were the cause, said truly, though it was not the sins he meant, but those which I have noticed. And as these were the sins of Princes, they it is who have paid the penalty.

But I desire to demonstrate still more clearly the untoward character of these forces. Captains of mercenaries are either able men or they are not. If they are, you cannot trust them, since they will always seek their own aggrandizement, either by overthrowing you who are their master, or by the overthrow of others contrary to your desire. On the other hand, if your captain be not an able man the chances are you will be ruined. And if it be said that whoever has arms in his hands will act in the same way whether he be a mercenary or no, I answer that when arms have to be employed by a Prince or a Republic, the Prince ought to go in person to take command as captain, the Republic should send one of her citizens, and if he prove incapable should change him, but if he prove capable should by the force of the laws confine him within proper bounds. And we see from experience that both Princes and Republics when they depend on their own arms have the greatest success, whereas from employing mercenaries nothing but loss results. Moreover, a Republic trusting to her own forces, is with greater difficulty than one which relies on foreign arms brought to yield obedience to a single citizen. Rome and Sparta remained for ages armed and free. The Swiss are at once the best armed and the freest people in the world.

Of mercenary arms in ancient times we have an example in the Carthaginians, who at the close of their first war with Rome, were well-nigh ruined by their hired troops, although these were commanded by Carthaginian citizens.[2] So too, when, on the death of Epaminondas, the Thebans made Philip of Macedon captain of their army, after gaining a victory for them, he deprived them of their liberty.[3] The Milanese, in like manner, when Duke Filippo died, took Francesco Sforza into their pay to conduct the war against the Venetians. But he, after defeating the enemy at Caravaggio, combined with them to overthrow the Milanese, his masters.[4] His father too while in the pay of Gio-

vanna, Queen of Naples, suddenly left her without
troops, obliging her, in order to save her kingdom, to
throw herself into the arms of the King of Aragon.

And if it be said that in times past the Venetians and
the Florentines have extended their dominions by
means of these arms, and that their captains have
served them faithfully, without seeking to make themselves their masters, I answer that in this respect the
Florentines have been fortunate, because among those
valiant captains who might have given them cause for
fear, some have not been victorious, some have had rivals, and some have turned their ambition in other di-
rections.

Among those not victorious, was Giovanni Acuto,
whose fidelity, since he was unsuccessful, was not put to
the proof: but any one may see, that had he been victorious the Florentines must have been entirely in his
hands.[5] The Sforzas, again, had constant rivals in the
Bracceschi, so that the one following was a check upon
the other; moreover, the ambition of Francesco was directed against Milan, while that of Braccio was directed
against the Church and the Kingdom of Naples. Let us
turn, however, to what took place lately. The Florentines chose for their captain Paolo Vitelli, a most prudent commander, who had raised himself from privacy
to the highest renown in arms. Had he been successful
in reducing Pisa, none can deny that the Florentines
would have been completely in his power, for they
would have been ruined had he gone over to their enemies, while if they retained him they must have submitted to his will.[6]

Again, as to the Venetians, if we consider the growth
of their power, it will be seen that they conducted their

affairs with glory and safety so long as their subjects of all ranks, gentle and simple alike, valiantly bore arms in their wars; as they did before they directed their enterprises landwards. But when they took to making war by land, they forsook those methods in which they excelled and were content to follow the customs of Italy.

At first, indeed, in extending their possessions on the mainland, having as yet but little territory and being held in high repute, they had not much to fear from their captains; but when their territories increased, which they did under Carmagnola,[7] they were taught their mistake. For as they had found him a most valiant and skilful leader when, under his command, they defeated the Duke of Milan, and, on the other hand, saw him slack in carrying on the war, they made up their minds that no further victories were to be had under him; and because, through fear of losing what they had gained, they could not discharge him, to secure themselves against him they were forced to put him to death. After him they have had for captains, Bartolommeo of Bergamo, Roberto of San Severino, the Count of Pitigliano, and the like, under whom their danger has not been from victories, but from defeats; as, for instance, at Vaila, where they lost in a single day what it had taken the efforts of eight hundred years to acquire. For the gains resulting from mercenary arms are slow, and late, and inconsiderable, but the losses sudden and astounding.

And since these examples have led me back to Italy, which for many years past has been defended by mercenary arms, I desire to go somewhat deeper into the matter, in order that the causes which led to the adoption of these arms being seen, they may the more readily be corrected. You are to understand, then, that when in these later times the Imperial control began to be rejected by Italy, and the temporal power of the Pope to be more thought of, Italy suddenly split up into a number of separate States. For many of the larger cities took up arms against their nobles, who, with the favour of the Emperor, had before kept them in subjection, and were supported by the Church with a view to add to her temporal authority: while in many others of these cities, private citizens became rulers. Hence Italy, having passed almost entirely into the hands of the Church and of certain Republics, the former made up of priests, the latter of citizens unfamiliar with arms, began to take foreigners into her pay.

The first who gave reputation to this service was Alberigo of Conio in Romagna, from whose school of warlike training descended,[8] among others, Braccio and Sforza, who in their time were the arbiters of Italy; after whom came all those others who down to the present hour have held similar commands, and to whose merits we owe it that our country has been overrun by Charles, plundered by Louis, wasted by Ferdinand, and insulted by the Swiss.

The first object of these mercenaries was to bring foot soldiers into disrepute, in order to enhance the merit of their own followers; and this they did, because lacking territory of their own and depending on their profession for their support, a few foot soldiers gave them no importance, while for a large number they were unable to provide. For these reasons they had recourse to horsemen, a less retinue of whom was thought to confer distinction, and could be more easily maintained. And the matter went to such a length, that in an army of twenty thousand men, not two thousand foot soldiers were to be found. Moreover, they spared no endeavour to relieve themselves and their men from fatigue and danger, not killing one another in battle, but making prisoners who were afterwards released without ransom. They would attack no town by night; those in towns would make no sortie by night against a besieging army. Their camps were without rampart or trench. They had no winter campaigns. All which arrangements were sanctioned by their military rules, contrived by them, as I have said already, to escape fatigue and danger; but the result of which has been to bring Italy into servitude and contempt.

Chapter XIII

OF AUXILIARY, MIXED, AND NATIONAL ARMS

❧

THE SECOND SORT of unprofitable arms are auxiliaries, by whom I mean, troops brought to help and protect you by a potentate whom you summon to your aid; as when in recent times, Pope Julius II observing the pitiful behaviour of his mercenaries at the enterprise of Ferrara, betook himself to auxiliaries, and arranged with Ferdinand of Spain to be supplied with horse and foot soldiers.[1]

Auxiliaries may be excellent and useful soldiers for themselves, but are always hurtful to him who calls them in; for if they are defeated, he is undone, if victorious, he becomes their prisoner. Ancient histories abound with instances of this, but I shall not pass from the example of Pope Julius, which is still fresh in men's minds. It was the height of rashness for him, in his eagerness to gain Ferrara, to throw himself without reserve into the arms of a stranger. Nevertheless, his good fortune came to his rescue, and he had not to reap the fruits of his ill-considered conduct. For after his auxiliaries were defeated at Ravenna, the Swiss suddenly descended and, to their own surprise and that of every one else, swept the victors out of the country,[2] so that, he neither remained a prisoner with his enemies, they being put to flight, nor with his auxiliaries, because victory was won by other arms than theirs. The Florentines, being wholly without soldiers of their own, brought ten thousand French men-at-arms to the siege of Pisa; thereby incurring greater peril than at any previous time of trouble.[3] To protect himself from his neighbours, the Emperor of Constantinople summoned ten thousand Turkish soldiers into Greece, who, when the war was over, refused to leave, and this was the beginning of the servitude of Greece to the Infidel.[4]

Let him, therefore, who would deprive himself of every chance of success, have recourse to auxiliaries, these being far more dangerous than mercenary arms, bringing ruin with them ready made. For they are united, and wholly under the control of their own officers; whereas, before mercenaries, even after gaining a victory, can do you hurt, longer time and better opportunities are needed; because, as they are made up of separate companies, raised and paid by you, he whom you place in command cannot at once acquire such authority over them as will be injurious to you. In short, with mercenaries your greatest danger is from their inertness and cowardice, with auxiliaries from their valour. Wise Princes, therefore, have always eschewed these arms, and trusted rather to their own, and have preferred defeat with the latter to victory with the former, counting that as no true victory which is gained by foreign aid.

I shall never hesitate to cite the example of Cesare

Borgia and his actions. He entered Romagna with a force of auxiliaries, all of them French men-at-arms, with whom he took Imola and Forli. But it appearing to him afterwards that these troops were not to be trusted, he had recourse to mercenaries from whom he thought there would be less danger, and took the Orsini and Vitelli into his pay. But finding these likewise while under his command to be fickle, false, and treacherous, he got rid of them, and fell back on troops of his own raising. And we may readily discern the difference between these various kinds of arms, by observing the different degrees of reputation in which the Duke stood while he depended upon the French alone, when he took the Orsini and Vitelli into his pay, and when he fell back on his own troops and his own resources; for we find his reputation always increasing, and that he was never so well thought of as when every one perceived him to be sole master of his own forces.

I am unwilling to leave these examples, drawn from what has taken place in Italy and in recent times; and yet I must not omit to notice the case of Hiero of Syracuse, who is one of those whom I have already named. He, as I have before related, being made captain of their armies by the Syracusans, saw at once that a force of mercenary soldiers, supplied by men resembling our Italian *condottieri*, was not serviceable; and as he would not retain and could not disband them, he caused them all to be cut to pieces and afterwards made war with native soldiers only, without other aid.[5]

And here I would call to mind a passage in the Old Testament as bearing on this point. When David offered himself to Saul to go forth and fight Goliath the Philistine champion, Saul to encourage him armed him with his own armour, which David, so soon as he had put it on, rejected, saying that with these untried arms he could not prevail, and that he chose rather to meet his enemy with only his sling and his sword. In a word, the armour of others is too wide, or too strait for us; it falls off us, or it weighs us down.[6]

Charles VII, the father of Louis XI, who by his good fortune and valour freed France from the English, saw this necessity of strengthening himself with a national army, and drew up ordinances regulating the service both of men-at-arms and of foot soldiers throughout his kingdom. But afterwards his son, King Louis, did away with the national infantry, and began to hire Swiss mercenaries. Which blunder having been followed by subsequent Princes, has been the cause, as the result shows, of the dangers into which the kingdom of France has fallen; for, by enhancing the reputation of the Swiss, the whole of the national troops of France have been deteriorated. For from their infantry being done away with, their men-at-arms are made wholly dependent on foreign assistance, and being accustomed to co-operate with the Swiss, have grown to think they can do nothing without them. Hence the French are no match for the Swiss, and without them cannot succeed against others.

The armies of France, then, are mixed, being partly national and partly mercenary. Armies thus composed are far superior to mere mercenaries or mere auxiliaries, but far inferior to forces purely national. And this example is in itself conclusive, for the realm of France would be invincible if the military ordinances of Charles VII had been retained and extended. But from want of foresight men make changes which relishing well at first do not betray their hidden venom, as I have already observed respecting hectic fever. Nevertheless, the ruler is not truly wise who cannot discern evils before they develop themselves, and this is a faculty given to few.

If we look for the causes which first led to the overthrow of the Roman Empire, they will be found to have had their source in the employment of Gothic mercenaries, for from that hour the strength of the Romans began to wane and all the virtue which went from them passed to the Goths. And, to be brief, I say that without national arms no Princedom is safe, but on the contrary is wholly dependent on Fortune, being without the strength that could defend it in adversity. And it has always been the deliberate opinion of the wise, that nothing is so infirm and fleeting as a reputation for power not founded upon a national army, by which I mean one composed of subjects, citizens, and dependants, all others being mercenary or auxiliary.

The methods to be followed for organizing a national army may readily be ascertained, if the rules above laid down by me, and by which I abide, be well considered, and attention be given to the manner in which Philip, father of Alexander the Great, and many other Princes and Republics have armed and disposed their forces.

Chapter XIV

OF THE DUTY OF A PRINCE IN RESPECT OF MILITARY AFFAIRS

———————⬥———————

A PRINCE, therefore, should have no care or thought but for war, and for the regulations and training it requires, and should apply himself exclusively to this as his peculiar province; for war is the sole art looked for in one who rules, and is of such efficacy that it not merely maintains those who are born Princes, but often enables men to rise to that eminence from a private station; while, on the other hand, we often see that when Princes devote themselves rather to pleasure than to arms, they lose their dominions. And as neglect of this art is the prime cause of such calamities, so to be a proficient in it is the surest way to acquire power. Francesco Sforza, from his renown in arms, rose from privacy to be Duke of Milan, while his descendants, seeking to avoid the hardships and fatigues of military life, from being Princes fell back into privacy. For among other causes of misfortune which your not being armed brings upon you, it makes you despised, and this is one of those reproaches, against which, as shall presently be explained, a Prince ought most carefully to guard.

Between an armed and an unarmed man no proportion holds, and it is contrary to reason to expect that the armed man should voluntarily submit to him who is unarmed, or that the unarmed man should stand secure among armed retainers. For with contempt on one side, and distrust on the other, it is impossible that men should work well together. Wherefore, as has already been said, a Prince who is ignorant of military affairs, besides other disadvantages, can neither be respected by his soldiers, nor can he trust them. A Prince, therefore, ought never to allow his attention to be diverted from warlike pursuits, and should occupy himself with them even more in peace than in war. This he can do in two ways, by practice or by study.

As to the practice, he ought, besides keeping his soldiers well trained and disciplined, to be constantly engaged in the chase, that he may inure his body to hardships and fatigue, and gain at the same time a knowledge of places, by observing how the mountains slope, the valleys open, and the plains spread; acquainting himself with the characters of rivers and marshes, and giving the greatest attention to this subject. Such knowledge is useful to him in two ways; for first, he learns thereby to know his own country, and to understand better how it may be defended; and next, from his familiar acquaintance with its localities, he readily comprehends the character of other districts when obliged to observe them for the first time. For the hills, valleys, plains, rivers, and marshes of Tuscany, for example, have a certain resemblance to those elsewhere; so that from a knowledge of the natural features of that province, similar knowledge in respect of other provinces may readily be gained. The Prince who is wanting in this kind of knowledge, is wanting in the first qualification of a good captain, for by it he is taught how to surprise an enemy, how to choose an encampment, how to lead his army on a march, how to array it for battle, and how to post it to the best advantage for a siege.

Among the commendations which Philopoemon,[1] Prince of the Achaians, has received from historians is this—that in times of peace he was always thinking of methods of warfare, so that when walking in the country with his friends he would often stop and talk with them on the subject. "If the enemy," he would say, "were posted on that hill, and we found ourselves here with our army, which of us would have the better position? How could we most safely and in the best order advance to meet them? If we had to retreat, what direction should we take? If they retired, how should we pursue?" In this way he put to his friends, as he went along, all the contingencies that can befall an army. He listened to their opinions, stated his own, and supported them with reasons; and from his being constantly occupied with such meditations, it resulted, that when in actual command no complication could ever present itself with which he was not prepared to deal.

As to the mental training of which we have spoken, a Prince should read histories, and in these should note the actions of great men, observe how they conducted themselves in their wars, and examine the causes of their victories and defeats, so as to avoid the latter and imitate them in the former. And above all, he should, as many great men of past ages have done, assume for his models those persons who before his time have been renowned and celebrated, whose deeds and achievements he should constantly keep in mind, as it is related that Alexander the Great sought to resemble Achilles, Cæsar Alexander, and Scipio Cyrus. And any one who reads the life of this last-named hero, written by Xenophon, recognizes afterwards in the life of Scipio, how much this imitation was the source of his glory, and how nearly in his chastity, affability, kindliness, and generosity, he conformed to the character of Cyrus as Xenophon describes it.

A wise Prince, therefore, should pursue such methods as these, never resting idle in times of peace, but strenuously seeking to turn them to account, so that he may derive strength from them in the hour of danger, and find himself ready should Fortune turn against him, to resist her blows.

Chapter XV

OF THE QUALITIES IN RESPECT OF WHICH MEN, AND MOST OF ALL PRINCES, ARE PRAISED OR BLAMED

———————⚜———————

IT NOW REMAINS for us to consider what ought to be the conduct and bearing of a Prince in relation to his subjects and friends. And since I know that many have written on this subject, I fear it may be thought presumptuous in me to write of it also; the more so, because in my treatment of it I depart from the views that others have taken.

But since it is my object to write what shall be useful to whosoever understands it, it seems to me better to follow the real truth of things than an imaginary view of them. For many Republics and Princedoms have been imagined that were never seen or known to exist in reality. And the manner in which we live, and that in which we ought to live, are things so wide asunder, that he who quits the one to betake himself to the other is more likely to destroy than to save himself; since any one who would act up to a perfect standard of goodness in everything, must be ruined among so many who are not good. It is essential, therefore, for a Prince who desires to maintain his position, to have learned how to be other than good, and to use or not to use his goodness as necessity requires.

Laying aside, therefore, all fanciful notions concerning a Prince, and considering those only that are true, I say that all men when they are spoken of, and Princes more than others from their being set so high, are characterized by some one of those qualities which attach either praise or blame. Thus one is accounted liberal, another miserly (which word I use, rather than *avaricious,* to denote the man who is too sparing of what is his own, *avarice* being the disposition to take wrongfully what is another's); one is generous, another greedy; one cruel, another tenderhearted; one is faithless, another true to his word; one effeminate and cowardly, another high-spirited and courageous; one is courteous, another haughty; one impure, another chaste; one simple, another crafty; one firm, another facile; one grave, another frivolous; one devout, another unbelieving; and the like. Every one, I know, will admit that it would be most laudable for a Prince to be endowed with all of the above qualities that are reckoned good; but since it is impossible for him to possess or constantly practise them all, the conditions of human nature not allowing it, he must be discreet enough to know how to avoid the infamy of those vices that would deprive him of his government, and, if possible, be on his guard also against those which might not deprive him of it; though if he cannot wholly restrain himself, he may with less scruple indulge in the latter. He need never hesitate, however, to incur the reproach of those vices without which his authority can hardly be preserved; for if he well consider the whole matter, he will find that there may be a line of conduct having the appearance of virtue, to follow which would be his ruin, and that there may be another course having the appearance of vice, by following which his safety and well-being are secured.

Chapter XVI

OF LIBERALITY AND MISERLINESS

—————◆—————

BEGINNING, THEN, with the first of the qualities above noticed, I say that it may be a good thing to be reputed liberal, but, nevertheless, that liberality without the reputation of it is hurtful; because, though it be worthily and rightly used, still if it be not known, you escape not the reproach of its opposite vice. Hence, to have credit for liberality with the world at large, you must neglect no circumstance of sumptuous display; the result being, that a Prince of a liberal disposition will consume his whole substance in things of this sort, and, after all, be obliged, if he would maintain his reputation for liberality, to burden his subjects with extraordinary taxes, and to resort to confiscations and all the other shifts whereby money is raised. But in this way he becomes hateful to his subjects, and growing impoverished is held in little esteem by any. So that in the end, having by his liberality offended many and obliged few, he is worse off than when he began, and is exposed to all his original dangers. Recognizing this, and endeavouring to retrace his steps, he at once incurs the infamy of miserliness.

A Prince, therefore, since he cannot without injury to himself practise the virtue of liberality so that it may be known, will not, if he be wise, greatly concern himself though he be called miserly. Because in time he will come to be regarded as more and more liberal, when it is seen that through his parsimony his revenues are sufficient; that he is able to defend himself against any who make war on him; that he can engage in enterprises against others without burdening his subjects; and thus exercise liberality towards all from whom he does not take, whose number is infinite, while he is miserly in respect of those only to whom he does not give, whose number is few.

In our own days we have seen no Princes accomplish great results save those who have been accounted miserly. All others have been ruined. Pope Julius II, after availing himself of his reputation for liberality to arrive at the Papacy, made no effort to preserve that reputation when making war on the King of France, but carried on all his numerous campaigns without levying from his subjects a single extraordinary tax, providing for the increased expenditure out of his long-continued savings. Had the present King of Spain been accounted liberal,[1] he never could have engaged or succeeded in so many enterprises.

A Prince, therefore, if he is enabled thereby to forbear from plundering his subjects, to defend himself, to escape poverty and contempt, and the necessity of becoming rapacious, ought to care little though he incur the reproach of miserliness, for this is one of those vices which enable him to reign.

And should any object that Cæsar by his liberality rose to power, and that many others have been advanced to the highest dignities from their having been liberal and so reputed, I reply, "Either you are already a Prince or you seek to become one; in the former case liberality is hurtful, in the latter it is very necessary that you be thought liberal; Cæsar was one of those who sought the sovereignty of Rome; but if after obtaining it he had lived on without retrenching his expenditure, he must have ruined the Empire." And if it be further urged that many Princes reputed to have been most liberal have achieved great things with their armies, I answer that a Prince spends either what belongs to himself and his subjects, or what belongs to others; and that in the former case he ought to be sparing, but in the latter ought not to refrain from any kind of liberality. Because for a Prince who leads his armies in person and maintains them by plunder, pillage, and forced contributions, dealing as he does with the property of others this liberality is necessary, since otherwise he would not be followed by his soldiers. Of what does not belong to you or to your subjects you should, therefore, be a lavish giver, as were Cyrus, Cæsar, and Alexander; for to be liberal with the property of others does not take from your reputation, but adds to it. What injures you is to give away what is your own. And there is no quality so self-destructive as liberality; for while you practise it you lose the means whereby it can be practised, and become poor and despised, or else, to avoid poverty, you become rapacious and hated. For liberality leads to one or other of these two results, against which, beyond all others, a Prince should guard.

Wherefore it is wiser to put up with the name of being miserly, which breeds ignominy, but without hate, than to be obliged, from the desire to be reckoned liberal, to incur the reproach of rapacity, which breeds hate as well as ignominy.

Chapter XVII

OF CRUELTY AND CLEMENCY, AND WHETHER IT IS BETTER TO BE LOVED OR FEARED

PASSING to the other qualities above referred to, I say that every Prince should desire to be accounted merciful and not cruel. Nevertheless, he should be on his guard against the abuse of this quality of mercy. Cesare Borgia was reputed cruel, yet his cruelty restored Romagna, united it, and brought it to order and obedience; so that if we look at things in their true light, it will be seen that he was in reality far more merciful than the people of Florence, who, to avoid the imputation of cruelty, suffered Pistoia to be torn to pieces by factions.[1]

A Prince should therefore disregard the reproach of being thought cruel where it enables him to keep his subjects united and obedient. For he who quells disorder by a very few signal examples will in the end be more merciful than he who from too great leniency permits things to take their course and so to result in rapine and bloodshed; for these hurt the whole State, whereas the severities of the Prince injure individuals only.

And for a new Prince, of all others, it is impossible to escape a name for cruelty, since new States are full of dangers. Wherefore Virgil, by the mouth of Dido, excuses the harshness of her reign on the plea that it was new, saying:

A fate unkind, and newness in my reign
Compel me thus to guard a wide domain.

Nevertheless, the new Prince should not be too ready of belief, nor too easily set in motion; nor should he himself be the first to raise alarms; but should so temper prudence with kindliness that too great confidence in others shall not throw him off his guard, nor groundless distrust render him insupportable.

And here comes in the question whether it is better to be loved rather than feared, or feared rather than loved. It might perhaps be answered that we should wish to be both; but since love and fear can hardly exist together, if we must choose between them, it is far safer to be feared than loved. For of men it may generally be affirmed that they are thankless, fickle, false, studious to avoid danger, greedy of gain, devoted to you while you are able to confer benefits upon them, and ready, as I said before, while danger is distant, to shed their blood, and sacrifice their property, their lives, and their children for you; but in the hour of need they turn against you. The Prince, therefore, who without otherwise securing himself builds wholly on their professions is undone. For the friendships which we buy with a price, and do not gain by greatness and nobility of character, though they be fairly earned are not made good, but fail us when we have occasion to use them.

Moreover, men are less careful how they offend him who makes himself loved than him who makes himself feared. For love is held by the tie of obligation, which, because men are a sorry breed, is broken on every whisper of private interest; but fear is bound by the apprehension of punishment which never relaxes its grasp.

Nevertheless a Prince should inspire fear in such a fashion that if he do not win love he may escape hate. For a man may very well be feared and yet not hated, and this will be the case so long as he does not meddle with the property or with the women of his citizens and subjects. And if constrained to put any to death, he should do so only when there is manifest cause or reasonable justification. But, above all, he must abstain from the property of others. For men will sooner forget the death of their father than the loss of their patrimony. Moreover, pretexts for confiscation are never to seek, and he who has once begun to live by rapine always finds reasons for taking what is not his; whereas reasons for shedding blood are fewer, and sooner exhausted.

But when a Prince is with his army, and has many soldiers under his command, he must needs disregard the reproach of cruelty, for without such a reputation in its Captain, no army can be held together or kept under any kind of control. Among other things remarkable in Hannibal this has been noted, that having a very great army, made up of men of many different nations and brought to fight in a foreign country, no dissension ever arose among the soldiers themselves, nor any mutiny against their leader, either in his good or in his evil fortunes. This we can only ascribe to the transcendent cruelty, which, joined with numberless great qualities, rendered him at once venerable and terrible in the eyes of his soldiers; for without this reputation for cruelty these other virtues would not have produced the like results.

Unreflecting writers, indeed, while they praise his achievements, have condemned the chief cause of them; but that his other merits would not by themselves have been so efficacious we may see from the case of Scipio, one of the greatest Captains, not of his own time only but of all times of which we have record, whose armies rose against him in Spain from no other cause than his too great leniency in allowing them a freedom inconsistent with military strictness. With which weakness Fabius Maximus taxed him in the Senate House, calling him the corrupter of the Roman soldiery. Again, when the Locrians were shamefully outraged by one of his lieutenants, he neither avenged them, nor punished the insolence of his officer; and this from the natural easiness of his disposition. So that it was said in the Senate by one who sought to excuse him, that there were many who knew better how to refrain from doing wrong themselves than how to correct the wrong-doing of others.[2] This temper, however, must in time have marred the name and fame even of Scipio, had he continued in it, and retained his command. But living as he did under the control of the Senate, this hurtful quality was not merely disguised, but came to be regarded as a glory.

Returning to the question of being loved or feared, I sum up by saying, that since his being loved depends upon his subjects, while his being feared depends upon himself, a wise Prince should build on what is his own, and not on what rests with others. Only, as I have said, he must do his utmost to escape hatred.

Chapter XVIII

How Princes Should Keep Faith

EVERY ONE understands how praiseworthy it is in a Prince to keep faith, and to live uprightly and not craftily. Nevertheless, we see from what has taken place in our own days that Princes who have set little store by their word, but have known how to overreach men by their cunning, have accomplished great things, and in the end got the better of those who trusted to honest dealing.

Be it known, then, that there are two ways of contending, one in accordance with the laws, the other by force; the first of which is proper to men, the second to beasts. But since the first method is often ineffectual, it becomes necessary to resort to the second. A Prince should, therefore, understand how to use well both the man and the beast. And this lesson has been covertly taught by the ancient writers, who relate how Achilles and many others of these old Princes were given over to be brought up and trained by Chiron the Centaur; since the only meaning of their having for instructor one who was half man and half beast is, that it is necessary for a Prince to know how to use both natures, and that the one without the other has no stability.

But since a Prince should know how to use the beast's nature wisely, he ought of beasts to choose both the lion and the fox; for the lion cannot guard himself from the toils, nor the fox from wolves. He must therefore be a fox to discern toils, and a lion to drive off wolves.

To rely wholly on the lion is unwise; and for this reason a prudent Prince neither can nor ought to keep his word when to keep it is hurtful to him and the causes which led him to pledge it are removed. If all men were good, this would not be good advice, but since they are dishonest and do not keep faith with you, you, in return, need not keep faith with them; and no Prince was ever at a loss for plausible reasons to cloak a breach of faith. Of this numberless recent instances could be given, and it might be shown how many solemn treaties and engagements have been rendered inoperative and idle through want of faith in Princes, and that he who was best known to play the fox has had the best success.

It is necessary, indeed, to put a good colour on this nature and to be skilful in simulating and dissembling. But men are so simple, and governed so absolutely by their present needs, that he who wishes to deceive will never fail in finding willing dupes. One recent example I will not omit. Pope Alexander VI had no care or thought but how to deceive, and always found material to work on. No man ever had a more effective manner of asseverating, or made promises with more solemn protestations, or observed them less. And yet, because he understood this side of human nature, his frauds always succeeded.

It is not essential, then, that a Prince should have all the good qualities which I have enumerated above, but it is most essential that he should seem to have them; I will even venture to affirm that if he has and invariably practises them all, they are hurtful, whereas the appearance of having them is useful. Thus, it is well to seem merciful, faithful, humane, religious, and upright, and also to be so; but the mind should remain so balanced that were it needful not to be so, you should be able and know how to change to the contrary.

And you are to understand that a Prince, and most of all a new Prince, cannot observe all those rules of conduct in respect whereof men are accounted good, being often forced, in order to preserve his Princedom, to act in opposition to good faith, charity, humanity, and religion. He must therefore keep his mind ready to shift as the winds and tides of Fortune turn, and, as I have already said, he ought not to quit good courses if he can help it, but should know how to follow evil courses if he must.

A Prince should therefore be very careful that nothing ever escapes his lips which is not replete with the five qualities above named, so that to see and hear him, one would think him the embodiment of mercy, good faith, integrity, humanity, and religion. And there is no virtue which it is more necessary for him to seem to possess than this last; because men in general judge rather by the eye than by the hand, for every one can see but few can touch. Every one sees what you seem, but few know what you are, and these few dare not oppose themselves to the opinion of the many who have the majesty of the State to back them up.

Moreover, in the actions of all men, and most of all of

Princes, where there is no tribunal to which we can appeal, we look to results. Wherefore if a Prince succeeds in establishing and maintaining his authority, the means will always be judged honourable and be approved by every one. For the vulgar are always taken by appearances and by results, and the world is made up of the vulgar, the few only finding room when the many have no longer ground to stand on.

A certain Prince of our own days, whose name it is as well not to mention,[1] is always preaching peace and good faith, although the mortal enemy of both; and both, had he practised them as he preaches them, would, oftener than once, have lost him his kingdom and authority.

Chapter XIX

THAT A PRINCE SHOULD SEEK TO ESCAPE CONTEMPT AND HATRED

HAVING NOW spoken of the chief of the qualities above referred to, the rest I shall dispose of briefly with these general remarks, that a Prince, as has already in part been said, should consider how he may avoid such courses as would make him hated or despised; and that whenever he succeeds in keeping clear of these, he has performed his part, and runs no risk though he incur other infamies.

A Prince, as I have said before, sooner becomes hated by being rapacious and by interfering with the property and with the women of his subjects, than in any other way. From these, therefore, he should abstain. For so long as neither their property nor their honour is touched, the mass of mankind live contentedly, and the Prince has only to cope with the ambition of a few, which can in many ways and easily be kept within bounds.

A Prince is despised when he is seen to be fickle, frivolous, effeminate, pusillanimous, or irresolute, against which defects he ought therefore most carefully to guard, striving so to bear himself that greatness, courage, wisdom, and strength may appear in all his actions. In his private dealings with his subjects his decisions should be irrevocable, and his reputation such that no one would dream of overreaching or cajoling him.

The Prince who inspires such an opinion of himself is greatly esteemed, and against one who is greatly esteemed conspiracy is difficult; nor, when he is known to be an excellent Prince and held in reverence by his subjects, will it be easy to attack him. For a Prince is exposed to two dangers, from within in respect of his subjects, from without in respect of foreign powers. Against the latter he will defend himself with good arms and good allies, and if he have good arms he will always have good allies; and when things are settled abroad, they will always be settled at home, unless disturbed by conspiracies; and even should there be hostility from without, if he has taken those measures, and has lived in the way I have recommended, and if he never abandons hope, he will withstand every attack; as I have said was done by Nabis the Spartan.

As regards his own subjects, when affairs are quiet abroad, he has to fear they may engage in secret plots; against which a Prince best secures himself when he escapes being hated or despised, and keeps on good terms with his people; and this, as I have already shown at length, it is essential he should do. Not to be hated or despised by the body of his subjects, is one of the surest safeguards that a Prince can have against conspiracy. For he who conspires always reckons on pleasing the people by putting the Prince to death; but when he sees that instead of pleasing he will offend them, he cannot summon courage to carry out his design. For the difficulties that attend conspirators are infinite, and we know from experience that while there have been many conspiracies, few of them have succeeded.

He who conspires cannot do so alone, nor can he assume as his companions any save those whom he believes to be discontented; but so soon as you impart your design to a discontented man, you supply him with the means of removing his discontent, since by betraying you he can procure for himself every advantage; so that seeing on the one hand certain gain, and on the other a doubtful and dangerous risk, he must either be a rare friend to you, or the mortal enemy of his Prince, if he keep your secret.

To put the matter shortly, I say that on the side of the conspirator there are distrust, jealousy, and dread of punishment to deter him, while on the side of the Prince there are the laws, the majesty of the throne, the protection of friends and of the government to defend him; to which if the general good-will of the people be added, it is hardly possible that any should be rash enough to conspire. For while in ordinary cases, the conspirator has ground for fear only before the execution of his villainy, in this case he has also cause to fear after the crime has been perpetrated, since he has the people for his enemy, and is thus cut off from every hope of shelter.

Of this, endless instances might be given, but I shall content myself with one that happened within the recollection of our fathers. Messer Annibale Bentivoglio, Lord of Bologna and grandfather of the present Messer Annibale, was conspired against and murdered by the Canneschi, leaving behind none belonging to him save

Messer Giovanni, then an infant in arms.[1] Immediately upon the murder, the people rose and put all the Canneschi to death. This resulted from the general goodwill with which the House of the Bentivogli was then regarded in Bologna; which feeling was so strong, that when upon the death of Messer Annibale no one was left who could govern the State, there being reason to believe that a descendant of the family (who up to that time had been thought to be the son of a smith) was living in Florence, the citizens of Bologna came there for him, and entrusted him with the government of their city; which he retained until Messer Giovanni was old enough to govern.

To be brief, a Prince has little to fear from conspiracies when his subjects are well disposed towards him; but when they are hostile and hold him in detestation, he has then reason to fear everything and every one. And well ordered States and wise Princes have provided with extreme care that the nobility shall not be driven to desperation, and that the commons shall be kept satisfied and contented; for this is one of the most important matters that a Prince has to look to.

Among the well ordered and governed Kingdoms of our day is that of France, wherein we find an infinite number of wise institutions, upon which depend the freedom and the security of the King, and of which the most important are the Parliament and its authority. For he who gave its constitution to this Realm, knowing the ambition and arrogance of the nobles, and judging it necessary to bridle and restrain them, and on the other hand knowing the hatred, originating in fear, entertained against them by the commons, and desiring that they should be safe, was unwilling that the responsibility for this should rest on the King; and to relieve him of the ill-will which he might incur with the nobles by favouring the commons, or with the commons by favouring the nobles, appointed a third party to be arbitrator, who without committing the King, might depress the nobles and uphold the commons. Nor could there be any better, wiser, or surer safeguard for the King and the Kingdom. And hence we may draw another notable lesson, namely, that Princes should devolve on others those matters that entail responsibility, and reserve to themselves those that relate to grace and favour. And again I say that a Prince should esteem the great, but must not make himself odious to the people.

To some it may perhaps appear, that if the lives and deaths of many of the Roman Emperors be considered, they offer examples opposed to the views expressed by me; since we find that some among them who had always lived good lives, and shown themselves possessed of great qualities, were nevertheless deposed and even put to death by their subjects who had conspired against them.

In answer to such objections, I shall examine the characters of several Emperors, and show that the causes of their downfall were in no way different from those which I have indicated. In doing this I shall submit for consideration such matters only as must strike every one who reads the history of these times; and it will be enough for my purpose to take those Emperors who reigned from the time of Marcus the Philosopher to the time of Maximinus, who were, inclusively, Marcus, Commodus his son, Pertinax, Julianus, Severus, Caracalla his son, Macrinus, Heliogabalus, Alexander, and Maximinus.

In the first place, then, we have to note that while in

other Princedoms the Prince has only to contend with the ambition of the nobles and the insubordination of the people, the Roman Emperors had a further difficulty to encounter in the cruelty and rapacity of their soldiers, which were so distracting as to cause the ruin of many of these Princes. For it was hardly possible for them to satisfy both the soldiers and the people; the latter loving peace and therefore preferring sober Princes, while the former preferred a Prince of a warlike spirit, however harsh, haughty, or rapacious; being willing that he should exercise these qualities against the people, as the means of procuring for themselves double pay, and indulging their greed and cruelty.

Whence it followed that those Emperors who had not inherited or won for themselves such authority as enabled them to keep both people and soldiers in check, were always ruined. The most of them, and those especially who came to the Empire new and without experience, seeing the difficulty of dealing with these conflicting humours; set themselves to satisfy the soldiers, and made little account of offending the people. And for them this was a necessary course to take; for as Princes cannot escape being hated by some, they should, in the first place, endeavour not to be hated by a class; failing in which, they must do all they can to escape the hatred of that class which is the stronger. Wherefore those Emperors who, by reason of their newness, stood in need of extraordinary support, sided with the soldiery rather than with the people; a course which turned out advantageous or otherwise, according as the Prince knew, or did not know, how to maintain his authority over them.

From the causes indicated it resulted that Marcus,

Pertinax, and Alexander, being Princes of a temperate disposition, lovers of justice, enemies of cruelty, gentle, and kindly, had all, save Marcus, an unhappy end. Marcus alone lived and died honoured in the highest degree; and this because he had succeeded to the Empire by right of inheritance, and not through the favour either of the soldiery or of the people; and also because, being endowed with many virtues which made him revered, he kept, while he lived, both factions within bounds, and was never either hated or despised.

But Pertinax was chosen Emperor against the will of the soldiery, who being accustomed to a licentious life under Commodus, could not tolerate the stricter discipline to which his successor sought to bring them back. And having thus made himself hated, and being at the same time despised by reason of his advanced age, he was ruined at the very outset of his reign.

And here it is to be noted that hatred is incurred as well on account of good actions as of bad; for which reason, as I have already said, a Prince who would maintain his authority is often compelled to be other than good. For when the class, be it the people, the soldiers, or the nobles, on whom you judge it necessary to rely for your support, is corrupt, you must needs adapt yourself to its humours, and satisfy these, in which case virtuous conduct will only prejudice you.

Let us now come to Alexander, who was so just a ruler that among the praises ascribed to him it is recorded, that, during the fourteen years he held the Empire, no man was ever put to death by him without trial. Nevertheless, being accounted effeminate, and thought to be governed by his mother, he fell into contempt, and the army conspiring against him, slew him.

When we turn to consider the characters of Commodus, Severus, and Caracalla, we find them all to have been most cruel and rapacious Princes, who to satisfy the soldiery, scrupled not to inflict every kind of wrong upon the people. And all of them, except Severus, came to a bad end. But in Severus there was such strength of character, that, keeping the soldiers his friends, he was able, although he oppressed the people, to reign on prosperously to the last; because his great qualities made him so admirable in the eyes both of the people and the soldiers, that the former remained in a manner amazed and awestruck, while the latter were respectful and contented.

And because his actions, for one who was a new Prince, were thus remarkable, I will point out shortly how well he understood to play the part both of the lion and of the fox, each of which natures, as I have observed before, a Prince should know how to assume.

Knowing the indolent disposition of the Emperor Julianus, Severus persuaded the army which he commanded in Illyria that it was their duty to go to Rome to avenge the death of Pertinax, who had been slain by the Pretorian guards. Under this pretext, and without disclosing his design on the Empire, he put his army in march, and reached Italy before it was known that he had set out. On his arrival in Rome, the Senate, through fear, elected him Emperor and put Julianus to death. After taking this first step, two obstacles still remained to his becoming sole master of the Empire; one in Asia, where Niger who commanded the armies of the East had caused himself to be proclaimed Emperor; the other in the West, where Albinus, who also aspired to the Empire, was in command. And as Severus judged it dangerous to declare open war against both, he resolved to proceed against Niger by arms, and against Albinus by artifice. To the latter, accordingly, he wrote, that having been chosen Emperor by the Senate, he desired to share the dignity with him; that he therefore sent him the title of Cæsar, and in accordance with a resolution of the Senate assumed him as his colleague. All which statements Albinus accepted as true. But so soon as Severus had defeated and slain Niger, and restored tranquillity in the East, returning to Rome he complained in the Senate that Albinus, all unmindful of the favours he had received from him, had treacherously sought to destroy him; for which cause he was compelled to go and punish his ingratitude. Whereupon he set forth to seek Albinus in Gaul, where he at once deprived him of his dignities and his life.

Whoever, therefore, examines carefully the actions of this Emperor, will find in him all the fierceness of the lion and all the craft of the fox, and will note how he was feared and respected by the people, yet not hated by the army, and will not be surprised that though a new man, he was able to maintain his hold of so great an Empire. For the splendour of his reputation always shielded him from the odium which the people might otherwise have conceived against him by reason of his cruelty and rapacity.[2]

Caracalla, his son, was likewise a man of great parts, endowed with qualities that made him admirable in the sight of the people, and endeared him to the army, being of a warlike spirit, most patient of fatigue, and contemning all luxury in food and every other effeminacy. Nevertheless, his ferocity and cruelty were so extravagant and unheard of (he having put to death a vast number of the inhabitants of Rome at different times, and the whole of those of Alexandria at a stroke), that he came to be detested by all the world, and so feared even by those whom he had about him, that at the last he was slain by a centurion in the midst of his army.

And here let it be noted that deaths like this which are the result of a deliberate and fixed resolve, cannot be escaped by Princes, since any one who disregards his own life can effect them. A Prince, however, needs the less to fear them as they are seldom attempted. The only precaution he can take is to avoid doing grave wrong to any of those who serve him, or whom he has near him as officers of his Court, a precaution which Caracalla neglected in putting to a shameful death the brother of this centurion, and in using daily threats against the man himself, whom he nevertheless retained as one of his bodyguard. This, as the event showed, was a rash and fatal course.

We come next to Commodus, who, as he took the Empire by hereditary right, ought to have held it with much ease. For being the son of Marcus, he had only to follow in his father's footsteps to content both the people and the soldiery. But being of a cruel and brutal nature, to sate his rapacity at the expense of the people, he sought support from the army, and indulged it in every kind of excess. On the other hand, by an utter disregard of his dignity, in frequently descending into the arena to fight with gladiators, and by other base acts wholly unworthy of the Imperial station, he became contemptible in the eyes of the soldiery; and being on the one hand hated, on the other despised, was at last conspired against and murdered.

The character of Maximinus remains to be touched

upon. He was of a very warlike disposition, and on the death of Alexander, of whom we have already spoken, was chosen Emperor by the army who had been displeased with the effeminacy of that Prince. But this dignity he did not long enjoy, since two causes concurred to render him at once odious and contemptible; the one the baseness of his origin, he having at one time herded sheep in Thrace, a fact well known to all, and which led all to look on him with disdain; the other that on being proclaimed Emperor, delaying to repair to Rome and enter on possession of the Imperial throne, he incurred the reputation of excessive cruelty by reason of the many atrocities perpetrated by his prefects in Rome and other parts of the Empire. The result was that the whole world, stirred at once with scorn of his mean birth and with the hatred which the dread of his ferocity inspired, combined against him, Africa leading the way, the Senate and people of Rome and the whole of Italy following. In which conspiracy his own army joined. For they, being engaged in the siege of Aquileja and finding difficulty in reducing it, disgusted with his cruelty, and less afraid of him when they saw so many against him, put him to death.

I need say nothing of Heliogabalus, Macrinus, or Julianus, all of whom being utterly despicable, came to a speedy downfall, but shall conclude these remarks by observing, that the Princes of our own days are less troubled with the difficulty of having to make constant efforts to keep their soldiers in good humour. For though they must treat them with some indulgence, the need for doing so is soon over, since none of these Princes possesses a standing army which, like the armies of the Roman Empire, has strengthened with the growth of his government and the administration of his State. And if it was then necessary to satisfy the soldiers rather than the people, because the soldiers were more powerful than the people, now it is more necessary for all Princes, except the Turk and the Soldan,[3] to satisfy the people rather than the soldiery, since the former are more powerful than the latter.

I except the Turk because he has always about him some twelve thousand foot soldiers and fifteen thousand horse, on whom depend the security and strength of his kingdom, and with whom he must needs keep on good terms, all regard for the people being subordinate. The government of the Soldan is similar, so that he too being wholly in the hands of his soldiers, must keep well with them without regard to the people.

And here you are to note that the State of the Soldan, while it is unlike all other Princedoms, resembles the Christian Pontificate in this, that it can neither be classed as new, nor as hereditary. For the sons of a Soldan who dies do not succeed to the kingdom as his heirs, but he who is elected to the post by those who have authority to make such elections. And this being the ancient and established order of things, the Princedom cannot be accounted new, since none of the difficulties that attend new Princedoms are found in it. For although the Prince be new, the institutions of the State are old, and are so contrived that the elected Prince is accepted as though he were an hereditary Sovereign.

But returning to the matter in hand, I say that whoever reflects on the above reasoning will see that either hatred or contempt was the ruin of the Emperors whom I have named; and will also understand how it happened that some taking one way and some the opposite, one only by each of these roads came to a happy, and all the rest to an unhappy end. Because for Pertinax and Alexander, they being new Princes, it was useless and hurtful to try to imitate Marcus, who was an hereditary Prince; and similarly for Caracalla, Commodus, and Maximinus it was a fatal error to imitate Severus, since they lacked the qualities that would have enabled them to tread in his footsteps.

In short, a Prince new to the Princedom cannot imitate the actions of Marcus, nor is it necessary that he should imitate all those of Severus; but he should borrow from Severus those parts of his conduct which are needed to serve as a foundation for his government, and from Marcus those suited to maintain it, and render it glorious when once established.

Chapter XX

WHETHER FORTRESSES, AND CERTAIN OTHER EXPEDIENTS TO WHICH PRINCES OFTEN HAVE RECOURSE, ARE PROFITABLE OR HURTFUL

TO GOVERN more securely some Princes have disarmed their subjects, others have kept the towns subject to them divided by factions; some have fostered hostility against themselves, others have sought to gain over those who at the beginning of their reign were looked on with suspicion; some have built fortresses, others have dismantled and destroyed them; and though no definite judgment can be pronounced respecting any of these methods, without regard to the special circumstances of the State to which it is proposed to apply them, I shall nevertheless speak of them in as comprehensive a way as the nature of the subject will admit.

It has never chanced that any new Prince has disarmed his subjects. On the contrary, when he has found them unarmed he has always armed them. For the arms thus provided become yours, those whom you suspected grow faithful, while those who were faithful at the first, continue so, and from your subjects become your partisans. And though all your subjects cannot be armed, yet if those of them whom you arm be treated with marked favour, you can deal more securely with the rest. For the difference which those whom you supply with arms perceive in their treatment, will bind them to you, while the others will excuse you, recognizing that those who incur greater risk and responsibility merit greater rewards. But by disarming, you at once give offence, since you show your subjects that you distrust them, either as doubting their courage, or as doubting their fidelity, each of which imputations begets hatred against you. Moreover, as you cannot maintain yourself without arms you must have recourse to mercenary troops. What these are I have already shown, but even if they were good, they could never avail to defend you, at once against powerful enemies abroad and against subjects whom you distrust. Wherefore, as I have said already, new Princes in new Princedoms have always provided for their being armed; and of instances of this History is full.

But when a Prince acquires a new State, which thus becomes joined on like a limb to his old possessions, he must disarm its inhabitants, except such of them as have taken part with him while he was acquiring it; and even these, as time and occasion serve, he should seek to render soft and effeminate; and he must so manage matters that all the arms of the new State shall be in the hands of his own soldiers who have served under him in his ancient dominions.

Our forefathers, even such among them as were esteemed wise, were wont to say that *Pistoia was to be held by feuds, and Pisa by fortresses,* and on this principle used to promote dissensions in various subject towns with a view to retain them with less effort. At a time when Italy was in some measure in equilibrium, this may have been a prudent course to follow; but at the present day it seems impossible to recommend it as a general rule of policy. For I do not believe that divisions purposely caused can ever lead to good; on the contrary, when an enemy approaches, divided cities are lost at once, for the weaker faction will always side with the invader, and the other will not be able to stand alone.

The Venetians, influenced as I believe by the reasons above mentioned, fostered the factions of Guelf and Ghibelline in the cities subject to them; and though they did not suffer blood to be shed, fomented their feuds, in order that the citizens having their minds occupied with these disputes might not conspire against them. But this, as we know, did not turn out to their advantage, for after their defeat at Vaila, one of the two factions, suddenly taking courage, deprived them of the whole of their territory.

Moreover methods like these argue weakness in a Prince, for under a strong government such divisions would never be permitted, since they are profitable only in time of peace as an expedient whereby subjects may be more easily managed; but when war breaks out their insufficiency is demonstrated.

Doubtless, Princes become great by vanquishing difficulties and opposition, and Fortune, on that account, when she desires to aggrandize a new Prince, who has more need than an hereditary Prince to win reputation, causes enemies to spring up, and urges them on to attack him, to the end that he may have opportunities to overcome them, and make his ascent by the very ladder which they have planted. For which reason, many are of the opinion that a wise Prince, when he has the occasion, ought dexterously to promote hostility to himself in certain quarters, in order that his greatness may be enhanced by crushing it.

Princes, and new Princes especially, have found greater fidelity and helpfulness in those whom, at the beginning of their reign, they have held in suspicion, than in those who at the outset have enjoyed their confidence; and Pandolfo Petrucci,[1] Lord of Siena, governed his State by the instrumentality of those whom he had at one time distrusted, in preference to all others. But on this point it is impossible to lay down any general rule, since the course to be followed varies with the circumstances. This only I will say, that those men who at the beginning of a reign have been hostile, if of a sort requiring support to maintain them, may always be won over by the Prince with much ease, and are the more bound to serve him faithfully because they know that they have to efface by their conduct the unfavourable impression he had formed of them; and in this way a Prince always obtains better help from them, than from those who serving him in too complete security neglect his affairs.

And since the subject suggests it, I must not fail to remind the Prince who acquires a new State through the favour of its inhabitants, to weigh well what were the causes which led those who favoured him to do so; and if it be seen that they have acted not from any natural affection for him, but merely out of discontent with the former government, that he will find the greatest difficulty in keeping them his friends, since it will be impossible for him to content them. Carefully considering the cause of this, with the aid of examples taken from times ancient and modern, he will perceive that it is far easier to secure the friendship of those who being satisfied with things as they stood, were for that very reason his enemies, than of those who sided with him and aided him in his usurpation only because they were discontented.

It has been customary for Princes, with a view to hold their dominions more securely, to build fortresses which might serve as a curb and restraint on such as have designs against them, and as a safe refuge against a first onset. I approve this custom, because it has been followed from the earliest times. Nevertheless, in our own days, Messer Niccolò Vitelli thought it prudent to dismantle two fortresses in Città di Castello in order to secure that town: and Guido Ubaldo, Duke of Urbino, on returning to his dominions, whence he had been driven by Cesare Borgia, razed to their foundations the fortresses throughout the Dukedom, judging that if these were removed, it would not again be so easily lost. A like course was followed by the Bentivogli on their return to Bologna.[2]

Fortresses, therefore, are useful or no, according to circumstances, and if in one way they benefit, in another they injure you. We may state the case thus: the Prince who is more afraid of his subjects than of strangers ought to build fortresses, while he who is more afraid of strangers than of his subjects, should leave them alone. The citadel built by Francesco Sforza in Milan, has been, and will hereafter prove to be, more dangerous to the House of Sforza than any other disorder of that State. So that, on the whole, the best fortress you can have, is in not being hated by your subjects. If they hate you no fortress will save you; for when once the people take up arms, foreigners are never wanting to assist them.

Within our own time it does not appear that fortresses have been of service to any Prince, unless to the Countess of Forlì after her husband Count Girolamo was murdered; for by this means she was able to escape the first onset of the insurgents, and awaiting succour from Milan, to recover her State; the circumstances of the times not allowing any foreigner to lend assistance to the people. But afterwards, when she was attacked by Cesare Borgia, and the people, out of hostility to her, took part with the invader, her fortresses were of little avail. So that, both on this and on the former occasion, it would have been safer for her to have had no fortresses, than to have had her subjects for enemies.

All which considerations taken into account, I shall applaud him who builds fortresses, and him who does not; but I shall blame him who, trusting in them, reckons it a light thing to be held in hatred by his people.

Chapter XXI

How a Prince Should Bear Himself So As to Acquire Reputation

━━━━━━━━━◆━━━━━━━━━

NOTHING MAKES a Prince so well thought of as to undertake great enterprises and give striking proofs of his capacity.

Among the Princes of our time Ferdinand of Aragon, the present King of Spain, may almost be accounted a new Prince, since from one of the weakest he has become, for fame and glory, the foremost King in Christendom. And if you consider his achievements you will find them all great and some extraordinary.

In the beginning of his reign he made war on Granada, which enterprise was the foundation of his power. At first he carried on the war leisurely, without fear of interruption, and kept the attention and thoughts of the Barons of Castile so completely occupied with it, that they had no time to think of changes at home. Meanwhile he insensibly acquired reputation among them and authority over them. With the money of the Church and of his subjects he was able to maintain his armies, and during the prolonged contest to lay the

foundations of that military discipline which afterwards
made him so famous. Moreover, to enable him to engage in still greater undertakings, always covering himself with the cloak of religion, he had recourse to what
may be called *pious cruelty*, in driving out and clearing
his Kingdom of the Moors;[1] than which exploit none
could be more wonderful or uncommon. Using the
same pretext he made war on Africa, invaded Italy, and
finally attacked France; and being thus constantly bus-
ied in planning and executing vast designs, he kept the
minds of his subjects in suspense and admiration, and
occupied with the results of his actions, which arose one
out of another in such close succession as left neither
time nor opportunity to oppose them.

Again, it greatly profits a Prince in conducting the internal government of his State, to follow striking methods, such as are recorded of Messer Bernabò of Milan,[2]
whenever the remarkable actions of any one in civil life,
whether for good or for evil, afford him occasion; and to
choose such ways of rewarding and punishing as cannot
fail to be much spoken of. But above all, he should
strive by all his actions to inspire a sense of his greatness
and goodness.

A Prince is likewise esteemed who is a stanch friend
and a thorough foe, that is to say, who without reserve
openly declares for one against another, this being always a more advantageous course than to stand neutral.
For supposing two of your powerful neighbours come
to blows, it must either be that you have, or have not,
reason to fear the one who comes off victorious. In either case it will always be well for you to declare yourself, and join in frankly with one side or other. For
should you fail to do so you are certain, in the former of

the cases put, to become the prey of the victor to the satisfaction and delight of the vanquished, and no reason or circumstance that you may plead will avail to shield or shelter you; for the victor dislikes doubtful friends, and such as will not help him at a pinch; and the vanquished will have nothing to say to you, since you would not share his fortunes sword in hand.

When Antiochus, at the instance of the Aetolians, passed into Greece in order to drive out the Romans, he sent envoys to the Achaians, who were friendly to the Romans, exhorting them to stand neutral. The Romans, on the other hand, urged them to take up arms on their behalf. The matter coming to be discussed in the Council of the Achaians, the legate of Antiochus again urged neutrality, whereupon the Roman envoy answered—"Nothing can be less to your advantage than the course which has been recommended as the best and most useful for your State, namely, to refrain from taking any part in our war, for by standing aloof you will gain neither favour nor fame, but remain the prize of the victor." And it will always happen that he who is not your friend will invite you to neutrality, while he who is your friend will call on you to declare yourself openly in arms. Irresolute Princes, to escape immediate danger, commonly follow the neutral path, in most instances to their destruction. But when you pronounce valiantly in favour of one side or other, if he to whom you give your adherence conquers, although he be powerful and you are at his mercy, still he is under obligations to you, and has become your friend; and none are so lost to shame as to destroy with manifest ingratitude, one who has helped them. Besides which, victories are never so complete that the victor can afford to disregard all considerations whatsoever, more especially considerations of justice. On the other hand, if he with whom you take part should lose, you will always be favourably regarded by him; while he can he will aid you, and you become his companion in a cause which may recover.

In the second case, namely, when both combatants are of such limited strength that whichever wins you have no cause to fear, it is all the more prudent for you to take a side, for you will then be ruining the one with the help of the other, who were he wise would endeavour to save him. If he whom you help conquers, he remains in your power, and with your aid he cannot but conquer.

And here let it be noted that a Prince should be careful never to join with one stronger than himself in attacking others, unless, as already said, he be driven to it by necessity. For if he whom you join prevails, you are at his mercy; and Princes, so far as in them lies, should avoid placing themselves at the mercy of others. The Venetians, although they might have declined the alliance, joined with France against the Duke of Milan, which brought about their ruin.[3] But when an alliance cannot be avoided, as was the case with the Florentines when the Pope and Spain together led their armies to attack Lombardy,[4] a Prince, for the reasons given, must take a side. Nor let it be supposed that any State can choose for itself a perfectly safe line of policy. On the contrary, it must reckon on every course which it may take being doubtful; for it happens in all human affairs that we never seek to escape one mischief without falling into another. Prudence therefore consists in knowing how to distinguish degrees of disadvantage, and in accepting a less evil as a good.

Again, a Prince should show himself a patron of merit, and should honour those who excel in every art. He ought accordingly to encourage his subjects by enabling them to pursue their callings, whether mercantile, agricultural, or any other, in security, so that this man shall not be deterred from beautifying his possessions from the apprehension that they may be taken from him, or that other refrain from opening a trade through fear of taxes; and he should provide rewards for those who desire so to employ themselves, and for all who are disposed in any way to add to the greatness of his City or State.

He ought, moreover, at suitable seasons of the year to entertain the people with festivals and shows. And because all cities are divided into guilds and companies, he should show attention to these societies, and sometimes take part in their meetings; offering an example of courtesy and munificence, but always maintaining the dignity of his station, which must under no circumstances be compromised.

Chapter XXII

OF THE SECRETARIES OF PRINCES

THE CHOICE of Ministers is a matter of no small moment to a Prince. Whether they shall be good or no depends on his prudence, so that the readiest conjecture we can form of the character and sagacity of a Prince, is from seeing what sort of men he has about him. When they are at once capable and faithful, we may always account him wise, since he has known to recognize their merit and to retain their fidelity. But if they be otherwise, we must pronounce unfavourably of him, since he has committed a first fault in making this selection.

There was none who knew Messer Antonio of Venafro as Minister of Pandolfo Petrucci, Lord of Siena, but thought Pandolfo a most prudent ruler in having him for his servant.[1] And since there are three scales of intelligence, one which understands by itself, a second which understands what is shown it by others, and a third which understands neither by itself nor on the showing of others, the first of which is most excellent, the second good, but the third worthless, we must needs admit that if Pandolfo was not in the first of these degrees, he was in the second; for when one has the judgment to discern the good from the bad in what another says or does, though he be devoid of invention, he can recognize the merits and demerits of his servant, and will commend the former while he corrects the latter. The servant cannot hope to deceive such a master, and will continue good.

As to how a Prince is to know his Minister, this unerring rule may be laid down. When you see a Minister thinking more of himself than of you, and in all his actions seeking his own ends, that man can never be a good Minister or one that you can trust. For he who has the charge of the State committed to him, ought not to think of himself, but only of his Prince, and should never bring to the notice of the latter what does not directly concern him. On the other hand, to keep his Minister good, the Prince should be considerate of him, dignifying him, enriching him, binding him to himself by benefits, and sharing with him the honours as well as the burthens of the State, so that the abundant honours and wealth bestowed upon him may divert him from seeking them at other hands; while the great responsibilities wherewith he is charged may lead him to dread change, knowing that he cannot stand alone without his master's support. When Prince and Minister are upon this footing they can mutually trust one another; but when the contrary is the case, it will always fare ill with one or other of them.

Chapter XXIII

THAT FLATTERERS SHOULD BE SHUNNED

ONE ERROR into which Princes, unless very prudent or very fortunate in their choice of friends, are apt to fall, is of so great importance that I must not pass it over. I mean in respect of flatterers. These abound in Courts, because men take such pleasure in their own concerns, and so deceive themselves with regard to them, that they can hardly escape this plague; while even in the effort to escape it there is risk of their incurring contempt.

For there is no way to guard against flattery but by letting it be seen that you take no offence in hearing the truth: but when every one is free to tell you the truth respect falls short. Wherefore a prudent Prince should follow a middle course, by choosing certain discreet men from among his subjects, and allowing them alone free leave to speak their minds on any matter on which he asks their opinion, and on none other. But he ought to ask their opinion on everything, and after hearing what they have to say, should reflect and judge for himself. And with these counsellors collectively, and with each of them separately, his bearing should be such, that each and all of them may know that the more freely they declare their thoughts the better they will be liked. Besides these, the Prince should hearken to no others, but should follow the course determined on, and afterwards adhere firmly to his resolves. Whoever acts otherwise is either undone by flatterers, or from continually vacillating as opinions vary, comes to be held in light esteem.

With reference to this matter, I shall cite a recent instance. Father Luke, who is attached to the Court of the present Emperor Maximilian, in speaking of his Majesty told me, that he seeks advice from none, yet never has his own way; and this from his following a course contrary to that above recommended. For being of a secret disposition, he never discloses his intentions to any, nor asks their opinion; and it is only when his plans are to be carried out that they begin to be discovered and known, and at the same time they begin to be thwarted by those he has about him, when he being facile gives way. Hence it happens that what he does one day, he undoes the next; that his wishes and designs are never fully ascertained; and that it is impossible to build on his resolves.

A Prince, therefore, ought always to take counsel, but at such times and seasons only as he himself pleases, and not when it pleases others; nay, he should discourage every one from obtruding advice on matters on which it is not sought. But he should be free in asking advice, and afterwards, as regards the matters on which he has asked it, a patient hearer of the truth, and even displeased should he perceive that any one, from whatever motive, keeps it back.

But those who think that every Prince who has a name for prudence owes it to the wise counsellors he has around him, and not to any merit of his own, are certainly mistaken; since it is an unerring rule and of universal application that a Prince who is not wise himself cannot be well advised by others, unless by chance he surrender himself to be wholly governed by some one adviser who happens to be supremely prudent; in which case he may, indeed, be well advised; but not for long, since such an adviser will soon deprive him of his Government. If he listen to a multitude of advisers, the Prince who is not wise will never have consistent counsels, nor will he know of himself how to reconcile them. Each of his counsellors will study his own advantage, and the Prince will be unable to detect or correct them. Nor could it well be otherwise, for men will always grow rogues on your hands unless they find themselves under a necessity to be honest.

Hence it follows that good counsels, whencesoever they come, have their origin in the prudence of the Prince, and not the prudence of the Prince in wise counsels.

Chapter XXIV

WHY THE PRINCES OF ITALY HAVE LOST THEIR STATES

THE LESSONS ABOVE taught if prudently followed will make a new Prince seem like an old one, and will soon seat him in his place more firmly and securely than if his authority had the sanction of time. For the actions of a new Prince are watched much more closely than those of an hereditary Prince; and when seen to be good are far more effectual than antiquity of blood in gaining men over and attaching them to his cause. For men are more nearly touched by things present than by things past, and when they find themselves well off as they are, enjoy their felicity and seek no further; nay, are ready to do their utmost in defence of the new Prince, provided he be not wanting to himself in other respects. In this way there accrues to him a twofold glory, in having laid the foundations of the new Princedom, and in having strengthened and adorned it with good laws and good arms, with faithful friends and great deeds; as, on the other hand, there is a double disgrace in one who has been born to a Princedom losing it by his own want of wisdom.

And if we contemplate those Lords who in our own times have lost their dominions in Italy, such as the King of Naples, the Duke of Milan, and others, in the first place we shall see, that in respect of arms they have, for reasons already dwelt on, been all alike defective;[1] and next, that some of them have either had the people against them, or if they have had the people with them, have not known how to secure themselves against their nobles. For without such defects as these, States powerful enough to keep an army in the field are never overthrown.

Philip of Macedon, not the father of Alexander the Great, but he who was vanquished by Titus Quintius, had no great State as compared with the strength of the Romans and Greeks who attacked him. Nevertheless, being a Prince of a warlike spirit, and skilful in gaining the good will of the people and in securing the fidelity of the nobles, he maintained himself for many years against his assailants, and in the end, though he lost some towns, succeeded in saving his Kingdom.[2]

Let those Princes of ours, therefore, who, after holding them for a length of years, have lost their dominions, blame not Fortune but their own inertness. For never having reflected in tranquil times that there might come a change (and it is human nature when the sea is calm not to think of storms), when adversity overtook them, they thought not of defence but only of escape, hoping that their people, disgusted with the arrogance of the conqueror, would some day recall them.

This course may be a good one to follow when all others fail, but it were the height of folly, trusting to it, to abandon every other; since none would wish to fall on the chance of some one else being found to lift him up. It may not happen that you are recalled by your people, or if it happen, it gives you no security. It is an ignoble resource, since it does not depend on you for its success; and those modes of defence are alone good, certain and lasting, which depend upon yourself and your own worth.

Chapter XXV

WHAT FORTUNE CAN EFFECT IN HUMAN AFFAIRS, AND HOW SHE MAY BE WITHSTOOD

✦

I AM NOT ignorant that many have been and are of the opinion that human affairs are so governed by Fortune and by God, that men cannot alter them by any prudence of theirs, and indeed have no remedy against them; and for this reason have come to think that it is not worth while to labour much about anything, but that they must leave everything to be determined by chance.[1]

Often when I turn the matter over, I am in part inclined to agree with this opinion, which has had the readier acceptance in our own times from the great changes in things which we have seen, and every day see happen contrary to all human expectation. Nevertheless, that our free will be not wholly set aside, I think it may be the case that Fortune is the mistress of one half our actions, and yet leaves the control of the other half, or a little less, to ourselves. And I would liken her to one of those wild torrents which, when angry, overflow the plains, sweep away trees and houses, and carry off soil from one bank to throw it down upon the other. Every one flees before them, and yields to their fury without the least power to resist. And yet, though this be their nature, it does not follow that in seasons of fair weather, men cannot, by constructing weirs and moles, take such precautions as will cause them when again in flood to pass off by some artificial channel, or at least prevent their course from being so uncontrolled and destructive. And so it is with Fortune, who displays her might where there is no organized strength to resist her, and directs her onset where she knows that there is neither barrier nor embankment to confine her.

And if you look at Italy, which has been at once the seat of these changes and their cause, you will perceive that it is a field without embankment or barrier. For if, like Germany, France, and Spain, it had been guarded with sufficient skill, this inundation, if it ever came upon us, would never have wrought the violent changes which we have witnessed.

This I think enough to say generally touching resistance to Fortune. But confining myself more closely to the matter in hand, I note that one day we see a Prince prospering and the next day overthrown, without detecting any change in his nature or character. This, I believe, comes chiefly from a cause already dwelt upon, namely, that a Prince who rests wholly on Fortune is ruined when she changes. Moreover, I believe that he will prosper most whose mode of acting best adapts itself to the character of the times; and conversely that he will be unprosperous, with whose mode of acting the times do not accord. For we see that men in these matters which lead to the end that each has before him, namely, glory and wealth, proceed by different ways, one with caution, another with impetuosity, one with violence, another with subtlety, one with patience, another with its contrary; and that by one or other of these different courses each may succeed.

Again, of two who act cautiously, you shall find that one attains his end, the other not, and that two of different temperament, the one cautious, the other impetuous, are equally successful. All which happens from no other cause than that the character of the times accords or does not accord with their methods of acting. And hence it comes, as I have already said, that two operating differently arrive at the same result, and two operating similarly, the one succeeds and the other not. On this likewise depend the vicissitudes of Fortune. For if to one who conducts himself with caution and patience, time and circumstances are propitious, so that his method of acting is good, he goes on prospering; but if these change he is ruined, because he does not change his method of acting.

For no man is found so prudent as to know how to adapt himself to these changes, both because he cannot deviate from the course to which nature inclines him, and because, having always prospered while adhering to one path, he cannot be persuaded that it would be well for him to forsake it. And so when occasion requires the cautious man to act impetuously, he cannot do so and is undone: whereas, had he changed his nature with time and circumstances, his fortune would have been unchanged.

Pope Julius II proceeded with impetuosity in all his undertakings, and found time and circumstances in such harmony with his mode of acting that he always obtained a happy result. Witness his first expedition against Bologna, when Messer Giovanni Bentivoglio was yet living.[2] The Venetians were not favourable to the enterprise; nor was the King of Spain. Negotiations respecting it with the King of France were still open. Nevertheless, the Pope with his wonted hardihood and impetuosity marched in person on the expedition, and by this movement brought the King of Spain and the Venetians to a check, the latter through fear, the former from his eagerness to recover the entire Kingdom of Naples; at the same time, he dragged after him the King of France, who, desiring to have the Pope for an ally in humbling the Venetians, on finding him already in motion saw that he could not refuse him his soldiers without openly offending him. By the impetuosity of his movements, therefore, Julius effected what no other Pontiff endowed with the highest human prudence could. For had he, as any other Pope would have done, put off his departure from Rome until terms had been settled and everything duly arranged, he never would have succeeded. For the King of France would have found a thousand pretexts to delay him, and the others would have menaced him with a thousand alarms. I shall not touch upon his other actions, which were all of a like character, and all of which had a happy issue, since the shortness of his life did not allow him to experience reverses. But if times had overtaken him, rendering a cautious line of conduct necessary, his ruin must have ensued, since he never could have departed from those methods to which nature inclined him.

To be brief, I say that since Fortune changes and men stand fixed in their old ways, they are prosperous so long as there is congruity between them, and the reverse when there is not. Of this, however, I am well persuaded, that it is better to be impetuous than cautious. For Fortune is a woman who to be kept under must be beaten and roughly handled; and we see that she suffers herself to be more readily mastered by those who so treat her than by those who are more timid in their approaches. And always, like a woman, she favours the young, because they are less scrupulous and fiercer, and command her with greater audacity.

Chapter XXVI

AN EXHORTATION TO LIBERATE ITALY FROM THE BARBARIANS[1]

━━━━━━━━━◆━━━━━━━━━

TURNING OVER in my mind all the matters which I have above been considered, and debating with myself whether in Italy at the present hour the times are such as might serve to confer honour on a new Prince, and whether a fit opportunity now offers for a prudent and valiant leader to bring about changes glorious for himself and beneficial to the whole Italian people, it seems to me that so many conditions combine to further such an enterprise, that I know of no time so favourable to it as the present. And if, as I have said, it was necessary in order to display the valour of Moses that the children of Israel should be slaves in Egypt, and to know the greatness and courage of Cyrus that the Persians should be oppressed by the Medes, and to illustrate the excellence of Theseus that the Athenians should be scattered and divided, so at this hour, to prove the worth of some Italian hero, it was required that Italy should be brought to her present abject condition, to be more a slave than the Hebrew, more oppressed than the Persian, more disunited than the Athenian, without a head, without order, beaten, spoiled, torn in pieces, over-run and abandoned to destruction in every shape.

But though, heretofore, glimmerings may have been discerned in this man or that, whence it might be conjectured that he was ordained by God for her redemption, nevertheless it has afterwards been seen in the further course of his actions that Fortune has disowned him;[2] so that our country, left almost without life, still waits to know who it is that is to heal her bruises, to put an end to the devastation and plunder of Lombardy, to the exactions and imposts of Naples and Tuscany, and to stanch those wounds of hers which long neglect has changed into running sores.

We see how she prays God to send some one to rescue her from these barbarous cruelties and oppressions. We see too how ready and eager she is to follow any standard were there only some one to raise it. But at present we see no one except in your illustrious House (pre-eminent by its virtues and good fortune, and favoured by God and by the Church whose headship it now holds), who could undertake the part of a deliverer.

But for you this will not be too hard a task, if you keep before your eyes the lives and actions of those whom I have named above. For although these men were singular and extraordinary, after all they were but men, not one of whom had so great an opportunity as now presents itself to you. For their undertakings were not more just than this, nor more easy, nor was God more their friend than yours. The justice of the cause is conspicuous; for that war is just which is necessary, and those arms are sacred from which we derive our only hope. Everywhere there is the strongest disposition to engage in this cause; and where the disposition is strong the difficulty cannot be great, provided you follow the methods observed by those whom I have set before you as models.

But further, we see here extraordinary and unexampled proofs of Divine favour. The sea has been divided; the cloud has attended you on your way; the rock has flowed with water; the manna has rained from heaven; everything has concurred to promote your greatness. What remains to be done must be done by you; since in order not to deprive us of our free will and such share of glory as belongs to us, God will not do everything himself.

Nor is it to be marvelled at if none of those Italians I have named has been able to effect what we hope to see effected by your illustrious House; or that amid so many revolutions and so many warlike movements it should always appear as though the military virtues of Italy were spent; for this comes from her old system being defective, and from no one being found among us capable to strike out a new. Nothing confers such honour on the reformer of a State, as do the new laws and institutions which he devises; for these when they stand on a solid basis and have a greatness in their scope, make him admired and venerated. And in Italy material is not wanting for improvement in every form. If the head be weak the limbs are strong, and we see daily in single combats, or where few are engaged, how superior are the strength, dexterity, and intelligence of Italians.[3] But when it comes to armies, they are nowhere, and this from no other reason than the defects of their leaders. For those who are skilful in arms will not obey, and every one thinks himself skilful, since hitherto we have had none among us so raised by merit or by fortune above his fellows that they should yield him the palm. And hence it happens that for the long period of twenty years, during which so many wars have taken place, whenever there has been an army purely Italian it has always been beaten. To this testify, first Taro, then Alessandria, Capua, Genoa, Vaila, Bologna, Mestri.

If then your illustrious House should seek to follow the example of those great men who have delivered their country in past ages, it is before all things necessary, as the true foundation of every such attempt, to be provided with national troops, since you can have no braver, truer, or more faithful soldiers; and although every single man of them be good, collectively they will be better, seeing themselves commanded by their own Prince, and honoured and esteemed by him. That you may be able, therefore, to defend yourself against the foreigner with Italian valour, the first step is to provide yourself with an army such as this.

And although the Swiss and the Spanish infantry are each esteemed formidable, there are yet defects in both, by reason of which troops trained on a different system might not merely withstand them, but be certain of defeating them. For the Spaniards cannot resist cavalry and the Swiss will give way before infantry if they find them as resolute as themselves at close quarters. Whence it has been seen, and may be seen again, that the Spaniards cannot sustain the onset of the French men-at-arms and that the Swiss are broken by the Spanish foot. And although of this last we have no complete instance, we have yet an indication of it in the battle of Ravenna, where the Spanish infantry confronted the German companies who have the same discipline as the Swiss; on which occasion the Spaniards by their agility and with the aid of their bucklers forced their way under the pikes, and stood ready to close with the Germans, who were no longer in a position to defend themselves; and had they not been charged by cavalry, they must have put the Germans to utter rout. Knowing, then, the defects of each of these kinds of troops, you can train your men on some different system, to withstand cavalry and not to fear infantry. To effect this, will not require the creation of any new forces, but simply a change in the discipline of the old. And these are matters in reforming which the new Prince acquires reputation and importance.

This opportunity then, for Italy at last to look on her deliverer, ought not to be allowed to pass away. With what love he would be received in all those Provinces which have suffered from the foreign inundation, with what thirst for vengeance, with what fixed fidelity, with what devotion, and what tears, no words of mine can declare. What gates would be closed against him? What people would refuse him obedience? What jealousy would stand in his way? What Italian but would yield him homage? This barbarian tyranny stinks in all nostrils.

Let your illustrious House therefore take upon itself this enterprise with all the courage and all the hopes with which a just cause is undertaken; so that under

your standard this our country may be ennobled, and
under your auspices be fulfilled the words of Petrarch:

> Brief will be the strife
> When valour arms against barbaric rage;
> For the bold spirit of the bygone age
> Still warms Italian hearts with life.[4]

NOTES

Dedication

1. **DEDICATION:** Machiavelli originally dedicated this book to Giuliano de' Medici. After Giuliano's death, he rededicated it to Lorenzo de' Medici, who assumed power. This form of dedication is an imitation of the ancient Greek authors. *The Prince* reads like a sort of letter to the ruler in power.

Chapter I

1. **Milan to Francesco Sforza:** Francesco Sforza (1401–66) was a mercenary, who had himself declared Duke of Milan in 1450.
2. **as the Kingdom of Naples:** The Kingdom of Naples had a confusing succession that left almost all of known Europe with some claim. The Treaty of Granada of 1500 partitioned the Kingdom between Spain and France until 1503—when King Ferdinand of Spain conquered it.

Chapter II

1. **having elsewhere spoken:** Machiavelli discusses republics in *Discourses on Livy's History*.
2. **Pope Julius in 1510:** Machiavelli describes Pope Julius's warlike character in detail in Chapter XXV.

Chapter III

1. **new ruler:** Ludovico Sforza first called the French into the Italian peninsula in 1494 in an attempt to assert Milan's claim on the Kingdom of Naples. Once the French armies invaded, however, they stayed, until the Spanish got involved a few years later.
2. **driven out of Italy:** After the French captured Milan for a second time, they held it for more than a a decade. It took Julius II's Lega Santa, a coalition of papal troops combined with those of Spain and Venice, with the support of England's Henry VIII and Holy Roman Emperor Maximilian I, to recover Milan.
3. **and Normandy:** Although Normandy was incorporated into France in 1204, the other provinces were absorbed over the last half of the fifteenth century.
4. **followed by the Turk:** The Turks captured Constantinople under Muhammad II in 1453 and stayed in power in Greece until 1832.
5. **by the Aetolians:** The Aetolians, a confederation of townships and rural communities in Greece, called in the Romans to help them against Philip V of Macedon. Unhappy with the support they received from Rome, the Aetolians ended up making peace with Philip.

6. **within that Province:** The Achaeans were a league of cities and communities. Antiochus III, King of Syria, invaded Greece in 196 B.C. The Romans defeated Antiochus at the Battle of Magnesia in Asia Minor in 190 B.C.

7. **longer possession of Italy:** Charles VIII of France, a weak, impractical ruler.

8. **more plainly seen:** Charles VIII dreamed of recapturing Constantinople and establishing French dominance in the region. The Italians joined with Maximilian I, the Holy Roman Emperor, to drive the French out.

9. **offering their friendship:** This list of Louis's friends included both powerful and not so powerful rulers. Machiavelli is pointing out that Louis misused the influence at his disposal.

10. **himself into Italy:** Pope Alexander VI was Roderigo Borgia, father of Cesare. The invading armies of France required the presence of King Louis XII because of the menacing presence of Cesare, backed by the pope, his father, in Rome.

11. **divide it with the king of Spain:** France had claims to the throne of Naples through Charles and the house of Anjou, but Naples was remote, and consequently hard to defend. The Treaty of Granada (1502) divided power in Naples between Spain and France, but Spain later took all of Naples for itself.

12. **effect his expulsion:** Instead of leaving Frederick of Aragon, the original ruler of Naples, in power but having ultimate control, Louis installed Ferdinand II, the Spanish king, who quickly had Louis expelled.

13. **of their dominions:** Louis joined with Julius II's League of Cambrai in 1508 to war against the Venetians, who had grown powerful. This proved to be a mistake, for once the Venetians were defeated, Julius II formed the Lega Santa, a coalition to rid Italy of the French. This coalition included the recently vanquished Venetians, who were angered at being attacked by the French.

14. **enterprise on his behalf:** The promise referred to here was made by Louis; he promised to help the Papal States secure the Romagna and to attack Naples in return for a sanctioned divorce from his wife, Jeanne, so he could marry Anne of Brittany and expand France's territory. The promise was made to Alexander VI but came back to haunt him when the clever and ambitious Julius II took over.

15. **occupying Romagna:** Machiavelli probably met George d'Amboise, the cardinal of Rouen, while on a diplomatic mission to France.

Chapter IV

1. **and mutual jealousies:** When Alexander the Great died suddenly in 323 B.C., his four top followers (Antipater, Antigonus, Ptolemy, and Perdiccas, later known collectively as the Diadochi) scrambled to seize power for themselves in a conflict known as the First Diadoch War. Their squabbles and battles lasted two generations and ultimately tore Alexander's great empire apart.

2. **changes at his pleasure:** Muhammad II ("the Conqueror," 1451–81), Sultan of Turkey, instituted an ef-

ficient centralized government. His successor Bayezid
II (1481–1512) continued Muhammad's work.

3. **some Baron of the Realm:** France was a place of
constant political intrigue, as various noblemen
schemed with foreign powers to increase their own
influence.

4. **nor that Pyrrhus:** Pyrrhus of Espirus was a great
military commander, but not a very good king. He
was unseated from his throne by a usurper when he
was seventeen. He managed to regain his throne a
few years later and sought to expand his power, but
despite his incredible military prowess, he lacked
the skill to hold territory once he won it. His name,
like Machiavelli's, has been turned into a common
phrase: a "pyrrhic victory" is a victory that costs the
victor dearly. The phrase derives from Pyrrhus's victory over the Romans at Ausculum in 279. He won,
but his army suffered massive casualties.

Chapter V

1. **lost them in the end:** In 405 B.C., the democracy
of Athens fell and was replaced by a Spartan oli-
garchy. In 382 B.C., a Spartan army occupied Thebes
and held it for three years.

2. **and never lost them:** The Romans captured
Capua in Italy (211 B.C.), Carthage in Africa (146
B.C.), and Numantia in Spain (133 B.C.) after lengthy
sieges, during which all three cities were destroyed.
Carthage and Numantia were both razed, and all
the conquered Capuans were sold into slavery.

3. **a hundred years of servitude:** Pisa was purchased
by Florence in 1405 and consequently subjugated.

After receiving cruel treatment for almost a hundred years, the Pisans asserted their liberty after the invasion by Charles VIII. The Florentines won it back in 1509.

Chapter VI

1. **Theseus, and the like:** Machiavelli uses as examples quasi-mythical heroes for his prince to use as models. All founded lasting civilizations.
2. **make unbelievers believe:** Savonarola's fall from power had more do to with the hostility of Pope Alexander VI and the House of Medici than lack of belief on the part of his followers.
3. **Prince of Syracuse:** Hiero II of Syracuse (306?–215 B.C.). A just and generous leader and a patron of the arts.

Chapter VII

1. **made princes by Darius:** Darius the Great (522?–486 B.C.), King of Persia, a strong, wise king who pursued a policy of expansion. Large sections of India became part of the Persian Empire under his rule.
2. **of the Orsini, and the Colonnesi:** The Orsini and Colonnesi were Roman families involved in a centuries-long feud.
3. **marriage of the French King:** Cesare Borgia was the legate who brought King Louis formal permission from the pope to divorce his first wife, Jeanne. This favor brought Louis under obligation to Pope Alexander and started a new round of international intrigues and wars on the Italian peninsula.

4. **enterprise against Romagna:** Cesare Borgia mounted two successful campaigns in the Romagna, a region in southeastern Italy.

5. **compelled him to desist:** Cesare Borgia continued his assault in the Romagna, and he took Urbino in 1502. Florence, sensing the danger, hired Cesare as protection for an expensive sum. The protection, of course, was from Cesare himself.

6. **mediation of Signor Paolo:** Signor Paolo is Paolo Orsini, head of the House of Orsini.

7. **his hands at Sinigaglia:** Vitellozzo Vitelli and Oliverotto da Fermo were strangled at Sinigaglia on the last day of December 1502. The Duke of Gravina and Paolo Orsini were executed a few days later.

8. **astounded and satisfied the populace:** Remirro de Orco was appointed lieutenant general of Romagna in March 1500. He was imprisoned on December 22, 1502, and put to death the day after Christmas.

9. **had Alexander lived:** Alexander VI died on August 18, 1503.

10. **protectorship of Pisa:** Pisa had declared itself independent and had relied on the French for support. But when the French were driven out by the Spaniards, only Cesare could restrain the Florentines from taking Pisa back.

11. **of any whom he disliked:** Pius III was elected as a compromise candidate. When he died, Giuliano della Rovere was elected with no competition and dubbed Julius II.

Chapter VIII

1. **be King of Syracuse:** A cruel tyrant of Syracuse, Agathocles (361–289 B.C.).

Chapter IX

1. **in Florence to Messer Giorgio Scali:** Tiberius and Gaius Gracchi, brothers, were popular Roman reformers of the second century B.C. They were murdered as a result of their resistance to the aristocracy and their unyielding reformist platform. Scali took part in the "revolt of the *ciompi*," an insurrection of the lower classes in Florence in 1378. He was beheaded after meeting with only brief success.

Chapter X

1. **regulations for their maintenance:** Florence sent Machiavelli as an emissary to the Holy Roman Emperor Maximilian I in 1507. Machiavelli traveled throughout Austria and later wrote a *Portrait of Things of Germany*.

Chapter XI

1. **and to crush the Venetians:** Julius II defeated the Venetians in 1509, then drove the French out of Italy with his Lega Santa in 1512.
2. **Alexander no one had followed:** Pope Alexander created cardinals and sold church offices on a grand scale to support his son Cesare's campaign in the Romagna, even pronouncing 1500 a jubilee year.

Pope Julius II followed this pattern of using church resources for material gain.

Chapter XII

1. **Italy with chalk:** Charles VIII conquered Italy "*col gesso,*" meaning "with chalk"—that is, without fighting. Pope Alexander VI supposedly remarked that Charles VIII invaded Italy so easily, he had no need to fight—he simply marked the houses he wanted for soldiers' quarters with chalk.
2. **commanded by Carthaginian citizens:** The "servile war" broke out in 241 B.C., after the First Punic War, when the Carthaginian mercenaries turned on their own masters.
3. **them of their liberty:** The Thebans were defeated by Philip of Macedon in the battle of Chaeronea (338 B.C.).
4. **the Milanese, his masters:** Duke Philip (1392–1447) was the last of the Visconti line. Three years later, Francesco Sforza, former supporter of the Visconti, declared himself Duke of Milan.
5. **in his hands:** Sir John Hawkwood (1320–94) of England was known as Giovanni Acuto and served the Florentines for many years with his "White Company."
6. **submitted to his will:** Paolo Vitelli commanded the Florentine mercenary armies against Pisa. He was eventually accused of treason and executed in 1499.
7. **under Carmagnola:** Francesco Bussone, Count of Carmagnola (1380–1432), led Florentine and Venetian forces against Milan in 1425. He did his

job with an apparently intentional lack of effectiveness. The Venetians had him tried and executed over his perceived betrayal.

8. **school of warlike training descended:** Alberigo de Barbiano, Count of Conio, founded the first Italian mercenary company and gave instruction on the art of mercenary warfare to many Italians, including Sforza the elder.

Chapter XIII

1. **horse and foot soldiers:** Julius II attacked Ferrara in 1510, using among other troops three hundred Spanish lances, supplied by Ferdinand.

2. **out of the country:** The French defeated the army of Pope Julius II at the Battle of Ravenna in 1512. Shortly thereafter, twenty thousand Swiss troops came to the rescue and forced the French to retreat.

3. **previous time of trouble:** In the summer of 1500, Gascon and Swiss mercenary troops mutinied against the Florentines for more pay.

4. **to the Infidel:** In 1353, Emperor John V Cantacuzene made the fatal error of inviting the Turks in to help defeat the Europeans. Once there, the Turks stayed.

5. **without other aid:** Hiero had to fight against a group of mercenaries called the Mamertines, originally hired by Agathocles, who threatened his rule of Syracuse. They had taken over the city of Messana and made themselves a nuisance by pirating and robbing throughout the area.

6. **weighs us down:** The biblical story of Saul and David can be found in I Samuel 17:29-39.

Chapter XIV

1. **Philopoemon:** Philopoemon (253–184 B.C.) was a leader of the Achaean league.

Chapter XVI

1. **accounted liberal:** King Louis XII, although eager for conquest, had a reputation for being a savvy money manager. King Ferdinand of Spain was equally prudent with money.

Chapter XVII

1. **to pieces by factions:** The incident referred to here involved two factions in the city of Pistoia, the Panciatichi and the Cancellieri. The Florentines, who were in control of the city, did not do anything to stop the conflict, and the Panciatichi and the Cancellieri massacred each other.
2. **wrong-doing of others:** Scipio captured the city of Locri in 205 B.C., and left it under the command of Pleminius, who occupied the city with brutal cruelty. His behavior caused a scandal, but Scipio was indifferent.

Chapter XVIII

1. **not well to mention:** The prince he does not name is most likely Ferdinand of Spain.

Chapter XIX

1. **an infant in arms:** Hannibal Bentivoglio was murdered in 1445. His son Giovanni was merely a young child at the time of his father's death.
2. **cruelty and rapacity:** Severus was a cruel despot who used loopholes in his own laws to kill and intimidate any who opposed him. His son Caracalla was worse, killing his brother Geta in his mother's arms then turning control of Rome over to her, spending the last bit of his life wandering the different military camps, until his own soldiers killed him.
3. **Turk and the Soldan:** By "the Turk," Machiavelli means the hereditary monarch of the Ottoman Empire. The "sultan" or "soldan" is the caliphate, established by the prophet Muhammad as an elected monarchy.

Chapter XX

1. **and Pandolfo Petrucci:** Pandolfo Petrucci (1451–1512) seized control of the government of Siena in 1487.
2. **on their return to Bologna:** In each of these instances, the destruction of the fortress was done for a different political reason. Bentivogli destroyed a castle built by Pope Julius II, destroying the emblem of his enemy's power. Niccolo, the father of Vitellozzo and Vitelli, destroyed the castles as a sign of confidence in his people. Guidobaldo, however, destroyed the fortresses because he discovered the hard way how useful they were to his enemies.
3. **subjects for enemies:** The Countess of Forlì was

Caterina Sforza, who had proven herself to be a tough, resourceful leader when she held onto a fortress after her husband died in 1488.

Chapter XXI

1. **his kingdom of the Moors:** Ferdinand expelled the Moors and the Jews from Spain, which deprived Spain of much of its artistic and cultural talent. His cruelty is pious, as he used religious (Catholic) rhetoric to fuel the action. Ferdinand used religious dogma to push much of his military activity, but it is clear that he did not believe in what he was saying, instead using people's faith as a political tool. At the time, the expulsion of the Moors and Jews was seen as a positive development; modern historians, however, point to it as one of Spain's big mistakes.
2. **Bernabò of Milan:** In the fourteenth century, Bernabò Visconti shared rule over Milan with his nephew, Gian Galeazzo.
3. **about their ruin:** This occurred in 1499, when Louis XII expelled Ludovico from Milan.
4. **to attack Lombardy:** Ferdinand and Julius II joined forces to drive the French out of Italy.

Chapter XXII

1. **in having him for a servant:** Antonio de Venafro was a lawyer who served Pandolfo Petrucci, the ruler of Siena.

Chapter XXIV

1. **been all alike defective:** Frederick of Aragon (the king of Naples) had no real chance of holding onto Naples. He was attacked by an alliance of the two greatest powers on the continent, Spain and France. And, being related to Ferdinand of Spain, he was unsuspecting of Ferdinand's treachery. However, the Duke of Milan, Ludovico Sforza, was a lazy, decadent, incompetent man, and his personal failings led to the loss of Milan to the French, who held it for years.
2. **succeeded in saving his Kingdom:** Philip V of Macedon (238–179 B.C.) fought two wars against the Romans, who were led by Titus Quintius Flamininus.

Chapter XXV

1. **everything to be determined by chance:** The idea of "Fortuna," or "fate," was a dominant force in Renaissance thinking, accepted as fact by the majority.
2. **Bentivoglio was yet living:** Pope Julius II attacked Baglioni of Perugia and Bentivoglio of Bologna in 1506 and quickly defeated both.

Chapter XXVI

1. **From the Barbarians:** This last chapter brings the book back to the dedication, as it is a plea to Lorenzo de'Medici to step into greatness and cast out the foreign invaders. Machiavelli lists all of Italy's major failures of recent times, before bombastically calling

for the Medicis to simultaneously free Italy from foreign influence and become the rulers of a new, unified country.

2. **Fortune has disowned him:** Cesare Borgia was on the verge of great success when he grew deathly ill and his father, Pope Alexander, died. This great misfortune prevented him from conquering Italy, thus unifying it.

3. **intelligence of Italians:** Machiavelli is referring to a famous hand-to-hand contest between Italy and France, wherein eleven Italians bested eleven Frenchmen. Italy took great pleasure in the news.

4. **Italian hearts with life:** Petrarch, canzone 128.

INTERPRETIVE NOTES

The Prince has been both maligned and praised for the past five centuries. It has been damned as immoral, brutal, violent, fascist, totalitarian, and godless and praised as satiric, humanistic, democratic, profound, and hopeful. Yet every critic agrees on one thing: the power of the clear, lucid prose Machiavelli employs. So how can an author everyone praises for writing so clearly be so hard to interpret? Was he a man obsessed with democratic ideals or an overly ambitious bureaucrat who wanted advancement any way he could get it? A realistic Christian or a hopeful atheist? A fierce republican or a dedicated fascist? Each reader must decide.

Handbook for Authoritarians?

In the paradigm presented in *The Prince,* humans are selfish animals ruled by base instincts and an insatiable desire to conquer, consume, and elevate themselves. Humans are not to be trusted. Humans are easily fooled. Humans are capable of great violence. Machiavelli held this human nature to be self-evident and unchanging, but saw a positive possibility in this dour worldview: Mankind, if effectively understood, could be organized, predicted, and catalogued. Human activity could be understood and molded, and a bright future built on these absolutes could be realized.

In *The Prince*, Machiavelli argues that conflict is the essence of political behavior. Rulers will always desire glory and other lands; generals will always desire to be rulers; soldiers will always desire to be generals; and civilians will always desire to be soldiers.

Conspiracies, purges, wars, revolutions, and any and all internal or external intrigues are business as usual in Machiavelli's political universe. The revolutionary aspect of his argument in *The Prince* is that he maintains that good can come out of violence, that stability can emerge from chaos, that tyranny can result in freedom, and that evil can produce good. He also argues that too much kindness and generosity in a ruler can actually have undesirable effects. Machiavelli convincingly establishes that a formidable ruler with a strong government can provide people with a society in which they can go about their lives with relative peace and freedom. He also shows that a weak government led by a meek prince is vulnerable to internal and external threats, which bring war and chaos. So, in the end, people are best served by the government of a tyrant.

The Ends and the Means

Machiavelli believed that history moved not in a forward progression, but in cycles. The virtues and failings of the past would continue to return, take root, and control the present. Machiavelli used past models as guides to future success. One of his main arguments, culled from these examples from ancient history, is that the end goal must be kept in mind when events begin to unfold.

Machiavelli does not, however, claim that any ends justify any means. He simply argues that a successful prince must sometimes act outside established religious or social mores. Machiavelli transposes nothing; the things men call good—honesty, charity, humility—are indeed good. And he separates many times the merely powerful from the truly great. But a strict adherence to a program of good deeds and virtue will not enable a prince to build a great, lasting society. As long as the goal is good enough, Machiavelli argues, violence and brutality cannot be wholly condemned. He uses the murder of Remus by Romulus in the establishment of Rome as an example. In this circumstance, a good, strong central government is created through an act of violence. Indeed, most readers can think of many examples from history in which violence or revolution have been instruments of positive change.

Machiavelli found the Christan virtues of meekness, kindness, suffering, and sacrifice to be righteous, but poor foundations for a strong central government. He preferred the earthier virtues of the ancient Roman era: courage, strength, and guile. Unswervingly Christian men, he argues, are easy prey for the ambitious, clever, unscrupulous, or cruel. To Machiavelli, political ineffectiveness was the ultimate vice in a prince.

Important Historical Figures

The Popes

Sixtus IV. He waged a war on the Florentines. To finance his military campaigns, he began the sale of indulgences and levied a new set of taxes on the faithful. He did much to beautify Rome. He started the building program that would include the Sistine Chapel. Sixtus IV was pope from 1471 to 1484.

Alexander VI. Like Sixtus, Alexander showered money on his relatives, but in his case, they were his illegitimate children. One of his illegitimate heirs was Cesare Borgia, who plays a central part in Machiavelli's book. Alexander and Cesare were ambitious enough to try to unify Italy under their rule. To do this, Alexander manipulated King Louis XII of France to back his son militarily. This plan backfired, however, as France stayed in the Italian peninsula. Alexander was pope from 1492 to 1503.

Julius II. This "warrior pope" led his armies personally. He bullied the other city-states to help him rid the peninsula of the French and pitted many of the major foreign powers against one another. This worked, but since he was old when elected to office, everyone knew he wouldn't live long. He hired Michelangelo to paint the ceiling of the Sistine Chapel. Julius II was pope from 1503 to 1513.

Spaniards

Francesco Sforza (1401–1466). Hired by the Visconti to protect Milan, Francesco Sforza, a soldier of fortune who supposedly could bend steel with his bare hands, turned against the Visconti and gained control of Milan. His rule was surprisingly moderate and led to a treaty with the Medicis in Florence. His successors, however, were overly ambitious or weak.

Ludovico Sforza (1451–1508). Son of Francesco, Ludovico Sforza's ambition exceeded his abilities. Although a patron of the arts (including Leonardo da Vinci), Ludovico invited France and Germany to become involved in Italian politics in 1494, hoping to reap the benefits himself. This proved to be a grave mistake, as it sparked a period of Italian unrest and invasions that lasted more than fifteen years.

Cesare Borgia (1475–1507). Cesare Borgia, illegitimate son of Pope Alexander VI, was a hard man in an age of hard men. Violent, cruel, and ambitious, he was a capable general and statesman who advanced his political career quickly through the influence of his father. Cesare's ambition was nothing less than to gain control of the whole of Italy. Just as it looked as if he could succeed, Pope Alexander VI died. Once Pope Julius II, an old enemy of the Borgias, took control of the Vatican, Cesare's ambitions were destroyed. Machiavelli apparently admired Borgia, as he heaps praise on him in *The Prince*; some critics, however, see this praise as ironic or satiric.

Foreign Monarchs

Charles VIII (1470–1498). Charles VIII began the long series of French invasions into Italy in 1494, where he decided, at the prompting of Ludovico Sforza, that Naples rightfully belonged to France. He suffered defeat in 1495 and retreated to France in debt. Passing through a doorway in 1498, he hit his head and fell into a coma, dying shortly thereafter.

Louis XII (1462–1515). Louis XII introduced reforms in the French tax system and was popular at home. In the footsteps of Charles VIII, he also led many invasions in Italy, beginning with the backing of Cesare Borgia in 1500. France took Milan and kept it for ten years. It was in Naples that the French and Spanish armies fell out, with the Spanish eventually winning. It took Pope Julius II's Lega Santa (holy league) to create a coalition of armies and kick the French out of Italy for good.

Ferdinand (1452–1516). King Ferdinand of Spain was a capable, greedy, manipulative ruler. He expelled the Moors and the Jews from Spain and took part in numerous wars. Ferdinand defeated France in Naples and received half of Naples' provinces in the Treaty of Granada, a treaty Ferdinand later broke. Spain ended up with all of Naples under its control. Ferdinand initiated the Spanish Inquisition and sent Christopher Columbus to the West Indies in 1492.

CRITICAL EXCERPTS

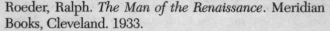

Roeder, Ralph. *The Man of the Renaissance*. Meridian Books, Cleveland. 1933.

Roeder highlights the lives of four Renaissance men in narrative fashion.

> The spirit of Cesare was indestructible: it was the spirit of Nature. His only sin was that he failed. The one occasion on which he was untrue to himself and trusted to the honour of others marked his downfall. But if the man failed, his method was sound; and the proof was that Julius [II] only overcame him by using it. . . . If Cesare was a lie, life was a lie; Nature was lawless, all men obeyed but one force—necessity. And that was the truth.

Durant, Will. *The Renaissance*. Simon and Schuster, New York. 1953.

An in-depth overview of Renaissance Italy.

It [Machiavelli's philosophy] is almost exclusively a political philosophy. There is no metaphysics here, no theism or atheism . . . ; and ethics itself is soon shoved aside as subordinate to, almost a tool of, politics. Politics he understands as the high art of creating, capturing, protecting, and strengthening a state. He is interested in states, rather than humanity. He sees individuals merely as members of a state; except as they help to determine its destiny, he pays no attention to the parade of egos across the landscape of time. He wishes to know why states rise and fall, and how they can be made to defer as long as possible to their inevitable decay.

Cropsey, Joseph, and Straus, Leo, eds. *History of Political Philosophy*. The University of Chicago Press, Chicago and London. 1963.

An in-depth look at the top thinkers in the field of political philosophy.

Machiavelli is not concerned with how men do live merely in order to describe it; his intention is rather, on the basis of knowledge of how men do live, to teach princes how they ought to rule and even how they ought to live. Accordingly, he rewrites, as it were, Aristotle's *Ethics*. To some extent he admits the traditional teaching is that men are obliged to live virtuously in the Aristotelian sense. But he denies that living virtuously is living happily or leads to happiness.

Raab, Felix. *The English Face of Machiavelli: A Changing Interpretation, 1500–1700*. Routledge & Kegan Paul, London. 1964.

Raab dissects Machiavelli while also showing the changing British critical response.

What is Machiavellianism? Is it the influence which the reading of Machiavelli's works exerts on practical men of affairs, and are the effects to be sought in actual political thought, to be assessed in terms of demonstrable familiarity with his writings? Or is it merely a generic, descriptive term applied to a certain kind of political thought and/or conduct, irrespective of direct contact with the writings of the man himself?

All these approaches are possible, though some are more possible than others. The study of his direct effect on political conduct is obviously dangerous ground—much of what may look like Machiavelli may not be Machiavelli but merely circumstantial necessity. "Generic" Machiavellianism, on the other hand, is perfectly acceptable, as long as it is made perfectly clear that the definition is the author's, and not Machiavelli's. Often, however, this is not done. Often all three approaches are lumped together without differentiation and it this which has led to the low level of Machiavelli studies today, relative to the general historical writing.

Mallett, Michael. *The Borgias: The Rise and Fall of a Renaissance Dynasty*. Barnes and Noble, Inc., New York. 1969.
Mallett examines the rise and fall of the Borgia family.

Machiavelli in *The Prince* claimed that the popularity and effectiveness of Cesare's rule was borne out by the way in which the Romagna cities remained faithful to him after his father's death. . . . On the other hand, it has been argued that the positive achievements of Borgia rule in the Romagna were almost nonexistent and that the population was terrified and discontented under ruthless and arbitrary rule.

Prescott, Orville. *Princes of the Renaissance*. Random House, New York. 1969.

Orville Prescott highlights the lives of many of the Renaissance princes and the philosophies that guided them.

All governments put one purpose before all others—to survive. To do so, all governments frequently violate standards of morality to which most individual men pay at least lip service. Recognizing these truths Niccolò Machiavelli expressed them bluntly in two celebrated books, *The Prince* and *Discourses on the First Ten Books of Livius*. Few books have provoked as much controversy and discussion as these. One reason for the unceasing debate is that Machiavelli had a split personality. At times he was a romantic reformer who yearned for virtue and morality; who idealized the peasants, who, he thought, would make fine soldiers; who believed in a republican form of government. He was deeply shocked by the corruption of the church.

At other times Machiavelli was a tough-minded observer of politics and power, a man who could take considerable relish in the brutal methods and artful schemes of the ruling princes. So some of his remarks reflect the hurt and dismay of the disillusioned idealist, some of the realist awareness of the dispassionate student of things as they are.

Bondanella, Peter, and Musa, Mark, eds. *The Portable Machiavelli*. Penguin Books, New York. 1979.
A collection of writings from Machiavelli, as well as interpretation and analysis.

While the weight of traditional critical opinion seems to favor the view that Machiavelli is the supreme realist, there is another current in recent criticism which stresses his literary and imaginative qualities: the impact of his prose style on his ideas; his creation of quasimythical characters from the raw materials of ancient or contemporary history; and the meaning of his particular political vocabulary. . . . No longer is Machiavelli treated as the author of a single, albeit very important, treatise on principalities. In remedying the traditional overemphasis on *The Prince*, recent criticism has also shifted attention to Machiavelli's role as a republican theorist and to his many original contributions in his analysis of the dynamics of political behavior in a self-governing body politic.

Berlin, Isaiah. *Against the Current: Essays in the History of Ideas*. Viking Press, New York. 1980.
Renowned essayist Isaiah Berlin writes of the people in history who moved against the popular currents of their day.

There is evidently something peculiarly disturbing about what Machiavelli said or implied, something that has caused profound and lasting uneasiness.

Modern scholars have pointed out certain real or apparent inconsistencies between the (for the most part) republican sentiment of *The Discourses* (and *The Histories*) and the advice to absolute rulers in *The Prince*; indeed there is a difference of tone between the two treatises, as well as chronological puzzles: this raises problems about Machiavelli's character, motives and convictions which for three hundred years and more have formed a rich field of investigation and speculation for literary and linguistic scholars, psychologists and historians.

Femia, Joseph. *The Machiavellian Legacy: Essays in Italian Political Thought*. University of Liverpool, Liverpool. 1998.
A collection of linked academic essays on Italian thinkers.

. . . As if anticipating Nietzsche, he [Machiavelli] levelled at Christianity the now familiar reproach of having made men humble, unmanly and feeble.

The Christian psychology of sin and redemption is nowhere to be found in his two major works. The idea of sin in Machiavelli has nothing in common with the idea of sin as breaking a commandment of God. Instead, "sins" are political errors, often committed by rulers who try to obey Christian ethics when objective circumstances require mercilessness or deception. Nor do we find the usual Christian imagery of divine and diabolic intervention in earthly affairs. He never invokes a supernatural will to explain the ultimate reason for things.

Viroli, Maurizio. *Niccolo's Smile: A Biography of Machiavelli*. Farrar, Straus, and Giroux, New York. 2000.

A new biography of Machiavelli that focuses on the life and mindset of Italy's most famous political philosopher.

What struck Machiavelli most was Germany's excellent military organization and the wealth of its communities and free cities. To be precise, he was impressed that they were wealthy because the populace lived in poverty. The German people, he wrote, "live like paupers"; they do not build, they do not spend money on garments, their larders are usually bare; they are happy to have bread, meat, and a "stove to ward off the cold."

. . . But the Florentines and Italians could learn a great deal from the Germans and Swiss in one area: Military organization. Their practices, he wrote, are admirable. They keep their soldiers "armed and well trained," just as he wished to do with the new Florentine militia.

QUESTIONS FOR DISCUSSION

Machiavelli's name has become synonymous with a certain type of amoral politics. After reading the text, do you believe the negative connotation of "Machiavellian" is deserved?

Why has *The Prince,* a short piece about a specific time in Italy's history, remained so widely read? What elements of the book make it relevant to new generations of readers? And does this slim little volume warrant centuries of attention?

Many political and corporate leaders in recent years have been accused of being "Machiavellian." Can you think of any figures to whom this term might apply? What makes them "Machiavellian"?

Some critics argued that, far from supporting totalitarianism, Machiavelli is satirizing it. Do you agree? If so, can you find examples from the text to support your opinion?

Is *The Prince* still relevant to today's leaders? In what ways can you see its influence, directly or otherwise, on current world affairs?

In what ways would Machiavelli have approved of the United States governmental system? In what ways would Machiavelli have disapproved?

Machiavelli saw history as a repeating sequence of cycles. In what ways is this true? Can you give examples that he himself would give if he were writing *The Prince* today?

Suggestions for the Interested Reader

If you enjoyed *The Prince*, you might also be interested in the following:

Family, by Mario Puzo. Puzo's (author of *The Godfather*) final novel (published in 2002), this is an exciting epic of the history of the Borgia family.

The Dream of Scipio, by Iain Pears. This fascinating, exciting 2002 novel juxtaposes events in three politically charged eras—the fall of the Roman Empire, the late Middle Ages, and the early years of World War II—and raises some difficult philosophical questions, among them "Do the ends justify the means?"

The New Machiavelli: The Art of Politics in Business, by Ian McAlpine. This 1999 book is one of the many in the past couple of generations to apply principles from Machiavelli's *The Prince* to the business world. It is funny and useful for current and future business people. Another such book is *What Would Machiavelli Do? The Ends Justify the Meanness* (2002) by Stanley Bing.

The Pope and the Heretic, by Michael White. White's 2002 biography of heretic Giordano Bruno offers a fascinating look at the time period of the Renaissance, and lays the intellectual and theological foundations from which the suffering of the period stemmed. White paints a layered, critical look at the church, at Italian politics, and mostly, at the pervasive damage done by the Inquisition.

FROM
POCKET BOOKS

THE SCARLET LETTER
Nathaniel Hawthorne
0-7434-8756-7
$3.95

THE ODYSSEY
Homer
0-671-01548-6
$5.99

THE PRINCE
Niccolo Machiavelli
0-7434-8768-0
$3.95

FRANKENSTEIN
Mary Shelley
0-7434-8758-3
$3.95

THE JUNGLE
Upton Sinclair
0-7434-8762-1
$5.95

UNCLE TOM'S CABIN
Harriet Beecher Stowe
0-7434-8766-4
$5.95

*ADVENTURES OF
HUCKLEBERRY FINN*
Mark Twain
0-7434-8757-5
$4.95

10210 (2 of 2)

For more information about the Enriched Classics program,
please visit www.simonsays.com.